WRITTEN REACTION

....

BY ELIOT WEINBERGER

AUTHOR

Works on Paper (1986)
19 Ways of Looking at Wang Wei (with Octavio Paz, 1987)
Outside Stories (1992)
Written Reaction: Poetics Politics Polemics (1996)

EDITOR

Montemora (1975-1982)
Una antología de la poesía norteamericana desde 1950 (1992)
American Poetry Since 1950: Innovators & Outsiders (1993)
Sulfur 33: Into the Past (1993)

EDITOR & TRANSLATOR

Octavio Paz, *Eagle or Sun?* (1970; new version, 1976)
Octavio Paz, *A Draft of Shadows* (1980)
Homero Aridjis, *Exaltation of Light* (1981)
Octavio Paz, *Selected Poems* (1984)
Jorge Luis Borges, *Seven Nights* (1984)
Octavio Paz, *Collected Poems 1957-1987* (1987)
Vicente Huidobro, *Altazor* (1988)
Octavio Paz, *A Tree Within* (1988)
Octavio Paz, *Sunstone* (1991)
Cecilia Vicuña, *Unravelling Words and the Weaving of Water* (1992)
Xavier Villaurrutia, *Nostalgia for Death* (1992)

Eliot Weinberger

WRITTEN REACTION

POETICS POLITICS POLEMICS

(1979-1995)

MARSILIO PUBLISHERS
NEW YORK

Most of these essays, in varying forms, originally appeared in the following periodicals and books: *Action Poétique* (France), *Agni*, *El Ángel* (Mexico), *Artes de México* (Mexico), *Global City Review*, *La Jornada Semanal* (Mexico), *The L.A. Weekly*, *Montemora*, *The Nation*, *Poetry Flash*, *Sibila* (Spain), *Sulfur*, *Vuelta* (Mexico); Eliot Weinberger, *Invenciones de papel* (Ediciones Vuelta, Mexico); Hugh MacDiarmid, *Selected Poems* (New Directions); *The Bread of Days: Eleven Mexican Poets Translated by Samuel Beckett* (Yolla Bolly); *Bronze Ages: Brian Nissen's Sculpture* (Clarion); *Contemporary Poets* (St. Martin's); *Octavio Paz: Los privilegios de la vista* (Centro Cultural/Arte Contemporáneo, Mexico); P. Joris, ed., *Joy! Praise! Jerome Rothenberg at 60* (Ta'wil); E.M. Santi, ed., *Archivo Blanco* (Ediciones del Equilibrista, Mexico). The essay "Paz in India" is a revised and expanded version of a text originally published in my book *Outside Stories* (New Directions).

Marsilio Publishers Corp.
853 Broadway
New York, NY 10003

Library of Congress Cataloging-in-Publication Data

Weinberger, Eliot
    Written reaction-poetics, politics, polemics/Eliot Weinberger.
        p.   cm.
    Includes index.
    ISBN 1-56886-027-7 (hardcover : alk. paper)
    I. Title
PS3573.E3928W75   1996
814' .54-dc20   96-755
                                                                CIP

Book design, Drentell Doyle Partners
Author photo by John Madere

Distributed in the United States by
Consortium Book Sales and Distribution
1045 Westgate Drive
Saint Paul, MN 55114

....

....

I used to live always in the beautiful Land of Poetry.
Then one day I found myself in Nonsense Land, and since then
I cannot find my way back home.

MAGGIE BROWNE,
The Book of Betty Barber (1900)

for N.S., A.D. *&* S.

CONTENTS

WRITTEN REACTION

[NOTE]

Nearly all the essays in this book are reactive: indignation, investigation, celebration, written in response to topics that were suggested by editors or merely happened to surface. Here, in loose chronological order, are reviews, notes, answers to questions, political commentary, introductions, informal talks, catalog texts, bits of autobiography, travel, literary history and natural history. Some of these were written for publication in Mexico and have never appeared in English; some are previously unpublished or obscurely published. The essays intended for specific magazines, particularly *Sulfur*, were written with a certain audience in mind; reprinting them here, I've not attempted to alter those contexts. The earliest pieces now remind me of Stendhal's injunction that one should enter society with a duel.

—E.W.

....

THIS BOOK WILL BE HERE

FOR A THOUSAND SECONDS

[*A review of Robert Bly,* This Tree Will Be Here for a Thousand Years *(Harper & Row), written for* The Nation, *1979. Bly, later the guru of the "men's consciousness" movement, was at the time engaged in an opposite pursuit: a promotion of the so-called "feminine" aspects of the American psyche.*]

R̲obert Bly is a windbag, a sentimentalist, a slob in the language. Yet he is one of the half-dozen living American poets who are widely read; and of them, the one whose work is most frequently imitated by fledgling poets and students of "creative writing." His success, however, is less disheartening when considered as an emblem of an age— perhaps the first in human history— where poetry is a useless pleasantry, largely ignored by the reading public.

In every pre-industrial society, the poet has played an essential role as prophet, chronicler, social and political commentator, singer, wit, refiner of the language, keeper of the myths. In the West, by the end of the 18th century, most of these functions had disappeared: the old myths had died in the mills and collieries; the rise of the novel and the newspaper (thanks in part to increased leisure time among the bourgeoisie, cheap methods of producing printed matter, global communication) replaced the necessity for the poem to narrate, chronicle, or comment on the world at large. The poets' response to this new irrelevancy was a turning inward toward secular exaltation: Romanticism.

Romanticism represented an exploration of what they imagined to be the passive, "feminine" aspect of human nature (which— need one say it?—is neither the exclusive nor general domain of women): moon, dream, shadow, sentiment, "the life of the mind" (as Wordsworth called his anti-epic), rhapsodies of the natural world. It was the creation of a counter-kingdom, a shadow government; the poet became the "unacknowledged legislator." The achievements of the few great poets of the time led to imitation and excess, and a new image— that of the moony poet— was petrified in the public mind. The adjective "poetic" became synonymous with *unworldly, dreamy, high-flown* (language), *sensitive*— in a word, *romantic*. "Poetic justice" meant that evil, in the end, would receive its just desert; a wishful contrast to political justice, which— as is evident in every issue of *The Nation*— is rarely so felicitous. The opposite of "poetic" became, naturally, "prosaic": *factual, down-to-earth*, at worst tedious as daily existence.

The revolution in American poetry at the beginning of the 20th century attempted to topple late Romanticism and return poetry to an active, self-consciously "masculine" position. At its worst, it meant ideology, like this from Ezra Pound in 1921: "Man really the phallus or spermatozoid charging, head-on the female chaos... Even oneself has felt it, driving any new idea into the great passive vulva of London." At its best, the poetry would incorporate politics, history, social comment, precise observation of the material world, urban topics, colloquial rather than "poetic" language, absolute concision of speech. The movement changed literature, yet failed, especially in America, to reinsert the poet into society: the old model held. For the last fifty years poetry has drifted even further from the mainstream, though important work still flourishes in the backwaters. Today poetry in the U.S. is a snail darter, a frobush lousewort: a frail, unimportant creature which is only visible when— as during the Vietnam War, for example— it becomes a nuisance, a slight hitch in the business at hand.

Meanwhile, a neo-Romantic poetry of noble sentiment continues to remain popular, especially among the young. It is sweet and escapist, like a so-called Gothic novel, and far from the world of the daily paper. "Disasters are all right," Robert Bly claims in his new collection, "if they teach men and women/ to turn their hollow places up." It is the language of Esalen, and not Bangladesh. Bly sees his mission as the restoration of the "feminine" to American poetry. (At his many public readings, he still stomps around the stage in a rubber LBJ mask, to symbolize "masculine"— meaning destructive— energy.) He has dismissed most of the North American masters (Pound, Williams, Eliot, et al) and has publicly knelt and kissed the hand of Pablo Neruda, his muse and role-model. Following Neruda, he has ignored musical structure and precision of language to exalt the image; imitating Neruda's imitation of Whitman, he has adopted the persona of the poet as the embracer of all beings: Bly's poems are a forest of exclamation marks, through which the phrase "I love" runs like an asylum escapee.

This Tree Will Be Here for a Thousand Years (48 poems which had previously appeared in 30 magazines) opens with a short essay on "The Two Presences." They are, according to Bly, the poet's own consciousness, which is "insecure, anxious, massive, earthbound, persistent, cunning, hopeful," and "the consciousness out there, in creatures and plants," which is, mercifully,

15

"none of these things," but which has "a melancholy tone." The poems, then, are an attempt to bridge this gap between inner and outer, and they do so by presenting an "I" whom we may assume is the poet himself, and a largely personified natural world. Not since Disney put gloves on a mouse has nature been so human: objects have "an inner grief"; alfalfa is "brave," a butterfly "joyful," dusk "half-drunk"; a star is "a stubborn man"; bark "calls to the rain"; "snow water glances up at the new moon." It's a carnival of pathetic fallacy. At times, Bly's all-embracing I, more childish than childlike, verges on the parodic: "I know no one on this train./ A man comes walking down the aisle./ I want to tell him/ that I forgive him, that I want him/ to forgive me." One longs for a new chapter to D.H. Lawrence's *Studies in Classical American Literature* ("Oh God! Better a bellyache. A bellyache is at least specific.")

Most college students who write poetry imitate Bly, not only because the poet's lack of emotional subtlety matches their own, but, most of all, because a Bly poem is so easy to write. Consider the first five lines of a poem in this collection called "Women We Never See Again":

There are women we love whom we never see again.
They are chestnuts shining in the rain.
Moths hatched in winter disappear behind books.
Sometimes when you put your hand into a hollow tree
you touch the dark places between the stars.

The first line flatly posits a familiar and "poetic" theme: lost love. The second sets up a metaphor that is entirely without meaning; any word could easily be replaced without altering the poem: they are Brazil nuts shining in the sun, they are Pontiacs idling in the moonlight, etc. The third line jumps to another unrelated image, and one that is probably inaccurate: the moths I know, at least, prefer the products of knit & purl to those of Harper & Row. Lines four and five, beginning with a wistful "sometimes," jump again, this time to a bit of fancy that might be charming if written by a third-grader. The poem, as all Bly poems, runs on, offering a new self-contained image every line or two, and then abruptly ends. What could be simpler for an adolescent— whose feelings cannot be restrained by technique— to copy?

Bly is a popular poet because his poems, to the general audience, sound like poems. The poet is identifiably cheery ("I loved that afternoon, and the rest of my life") or sad ("In a few years we will die") and his images have all been certified as "poetic": snow, moon, lakes, trees, shadows, horses, birds, night, rain, wind, lions, graves and so on. That his enthusiasm is expressed through pointless and rarely believable metaphor— who else would compare the sound of a cricket to a sailboat?—that his facility for English seems to have been warped by reading (and writing) too many bad translations, that he has never conceived of the line as a unit of musical measure, are subtleties that are largely lost to the college crowds. That a bad poet is widely read is hardly news. What is disturbing, however, is the fact that so many young writers— who should be experimental, wild, outraged, idealistic— are modeling themselves after this utterly safe, cozily irrelevant poet, a man who has written, with numbing sincerity, "It is good to be poor, and to listen to the wind."

[*Postscript, 1995*: Bly's relaxed surrealism has now been largely replaced, in the writing schools, by "realist" description and auto-therapy.]

PEGASUS AT THE GLUE FACTORY

[*A review of* The Poetry Anthology 1912-1977, *edited by*
Daryl Hine & Joseph Parisi (Houghton Mifflin),
written for Montemora, 1979.]

Daryl Hine took America's most successful and prestigious poetry magazine and drove it to ruin. Yet far more reprehensible is the continuing campaign of vilification he has directed against his predecessor, the late Henry Rago.

After the death of Harriet Monroe in 1936, *Poetry* drifted for nineteen years in a vapid succession of short-term editors and editorial committees. By 1955, when Rago assumed the editorship, the magazine was in a state of financial collapse. A strict organizer— even specifying the brand of office paper clips— he quickly brought *Poetry* into the period of its greatest prosperity. More significant, he heeded Eliot's advice that *Poetry* was an institution, not a little magazine. It existed not to promote a specific group or genre, but rather to display monthly the range of the serious writing that occurred in the country. Neither fief nor commune, *Poetry* was, ideally, the Republic of Letters.

The history of *Poetry* and its editors is encapsuled in the evolution of the magazine's cover. Rago's restoration of the Monroe

Pegasus, now in a tasteful sketch, the grand procession of monthly colors, and the sober list of contributors all reflected his editorial intent. This was the real thing, Mt. Olympus, high above the warring factions. Almost every poet of interest, from all fronts, was represented, and entry became a rite of initiation for the young. A debut in *Poetry* was admission to the Guild, a license to practice. (Today, there is nothing remotely similar, only a nod from the creative writing school teacher.)

On May 18, 1969, Daryl Hine was announced as Rago's successor, and eleven days later Rago's heart gave out. The magazine changed immediately. The tell-tale cover eliminated Pegasus and the poets, and gave its entire space to doleful pen-and-inks: On the outside, Poetry had become the Pawpaw College Lit. Mag. Inside was equally grim: Hine's 57 varieties of studied irony, a lugubrious murmur of "Sewanee, how I love you..." Within a year and a half, circulation had fallen nearly 20%, indicating a drop in individual subscriptions and sales (libraries generally renew automatically). The magazine began to lose money seriously, and even the *Reader's Guide to Periodical Literature* (which had been indexing *Poetry* since 1915) dropped them, resulting in a further loss of subscriptions, now from the smaller libraries.

In 1978, after nine drooping years, Hine finally stepped down. His chosen replacement— inspired, perhaps, by Tutmania— was a member of the editorial committee of the 1940's, John Frederick Nims, the man who once compared the *Cantos* to cancer cells. His first act was to restore the Rago cover, but with one significant change: the grave and graceful Rago Pegasus was now a cute winged horsey drawn by James Thurber. As all institutions in the final stage of decay, *Poetry* had become a parody of itself.

The Poetry Anthology purports to represent "sixty-five years of America's most distinguished magazine." A judicious anthologist would have attempted to mirror each succeeding editor's taste. Hine & Parisi, however, shamelessly offer their own claustrophobic reading of literary history. Scores of regular contributors— in the style of the Soviet Encyclopedia— have mysteriously vanished.

Examine, for example, four typical Rago years: April 1965 to March 1969 (all of Volumes 106 through 113). The following were among the avant-gardist poets published, often in long selections and often repeatedly, alongside the traditionalist practitioners: Antin; Blackburn; Bowering; Bromige; Bunting (the complete *Briggflatts*); Creeley; Davenport; Dorn; Dull; Duncan (including some particularly fine "Passages"); Eigner; Enslin; Eshleman; Hollo; Irby; Ronald Johnson; Levertov; Loewinsohn; Merton; Stuart Montgomery (the complete *Circe*); Niedecker; Olson (from *Maximus*); Oppen; Rakosi; Margaret Randall; Raworth; Tim Reynolds; Rexroth; Rukeyser; Samperi; even Aram Saroyan; Silliman; Snyder; Sorrentino; Tomlinson; Turnbull; Whalen; Zukofsky (including special issues and the complete *"A"-14, 15, 18, 19, 21*).

Hine & Parisi give sixteen anthology pages to those four years. (110 of the book's 520 pages are devoted to eight of Hine's years as editor.) The poets chosen from that period are Carruth, Sexton, Snyder, Van Duyn, Tomlinson (twice), Spacks, Hollander (a little poem in the shape of a swan...), Howard, Stafford, W.S. Graham, Benedikt, Bly, Merwin, Karl Shapiro, Winfield Townley Scott, Mark Van Doren and Vernon Watkins. Althoughmany from the first list were *Poetry* regulars, a search elsewhere in the anthology is equally depressing. Some are grudgingly allotted one poem each, despite long associations with the magazine. Some, like Bunting and Zukofsky, are represented by a few early poems, but nothing from *Briggflatts* or *The Spoils*— first published in *Poetry*— or *"A"*, which the magazine practically serialized over forty years. Others, like Olson and Rexroth, have simply vanished, while immortals like David Wagoner, John Ciardi, and Turner Cassity are given multiple entries.

Nor is Hine's distaste for Rago and his policies limited to editorial subversion. In a 13-page introduction, the fourteen Rago years are discussed and dismissed in one paragraph: "He seems, from the space he gave certain fashionable poets both in the magazine and on its movie-marquee-like cover, to have picked favorites...there were few surprises in these years." (Earlier, Hine notes that Ezra Pound's "influence on *Poetry*, as on modern poetry in general, has been exaggerated out of proportion...") Revisionism has even oozed on to the book's dust jacket: 33 snapshots of poets and editors, but no Rago and no Pound. Worse, the fat spine is adorned with a goony freshman Thom Gunn, a marcelled Randall Jarrell, and a squishy Amy Lowell. They stare from the shelf.

As *Poetry* (Hine) had few readers, and as only collecting completists would consider buying this book, a dutiful reviewer should provide a brief synopsis of this last decade. A few titles and the first lines of poems tell it all: Like a particularly damp provincial museum, the pages were crowded with plaster-casts: "Baucis and Philomen"; "Dido: Swarming"; "Muse"; "Credo"; "Pervigilium Veneris"; "Death & Empedocles" and "Empedocles on Etna" (by different authors); "Narcissus to Himself"; "Satyr"; "Bird and the Muse"; "Homage to the Caracci." There was some tourism, but no exotic climes: "Hotel in Paris"; "Circumambulation of Mt. Tamalpais"; "Stones: Avesbury"; "Historical Museum, Manitoulin Island"; "Winter Drive"; "Leaving Buffalo"; "Under the Arc de Triomphe October 17" (which begins "The French clocks struck two-thirty"); "Wandsworth Common." There were "Waiting Rooms" ("What great genius invented the waiting

21

room?") and "The Waiting Room" ("I sit thinking of a rowing-boat I saw"). There was introspection: "The world is several billion years of age/ and I am thirty"; "What of these verses that I write"; "I attended the burial of all my rosy feelings"; I was always called in early for dinner." There was observation ("Night is a black swan"); ruminations on poetry ("The old forms are like birdhouses") and on gastronomy ("The Joy of Cooking"; "Twinings Orange Pekoe"). And no end to freshman wit: "Vowel Movements" (that one, five pages long, by Hine himself); "The Poet's Farewell to His Teeth."

The Hine section is swiftly read, for only those in solitary confinement with only this book could get past most of the first lines. And yet, three whole lines, the opening of a poem called "The Pleasure of Ruins," are worthy of citation for their spectacular kitsch:

> We cannot walk like Byron among Ayasoluk's ruined
> mosques, kicking the heads off yellow iris and eating
> cold lamb, but still we never envy the Bedouin.

But hold, reader: four more opening lines, and then good night:

> Reading through your work tonight
> As though it were autobiography
> I find your resonance... [author's ellipsis]
> "I shan't be yours forever; even this can't last."

....

GRIFFIN: RUIN'S VERGE

[Written as the entry on Jonathan Griffin for the reference book,
Contemporary Poets *(St. Martin's), 1979.]*

The card catalogue of the New York Public Library assumes that there are three Jonathan Griffins: the English poet, the 1930's journalist and expert on military affairs, and the translator of a shelf-full of books from seven European languages. To these we might add the "would-be" pianist who studied with Schnabel in Berlin in the early 1930's, the director of BBC European Intelligence during World War II, the diplomat in Paris, the screenwriter in Rome, the playwright featured at the Edinburgh Festival in 1957. But amidst this flock of public Griffins, the poet— the one whose work will last— has scarcely been visible. Until quite recently the poems rarely appeared in magazines, and his books were published by the smallest of small presses. Today one can find Griffin, if one looks hard enough, but there has been no critical attention paid him, other than a few short reviews. One poem was anthologized once; no survey of contemporary writing has even mentioned his name. He is, in short, that hidden treasure, a poet's poet's poet.

The voice is unique, and even at first glance a Griffin poem is unmistakable: titles which seem to come from nowhere ("You

May Come Out"; "Ear to House—"; "3 Angels in Supernova"; "Into the Straight"; "At the Crucifixion of One's Heirs"; "The World is Bugged"); rhymes that appear and disappear; neologisms (*breathprint, terracide, gravechill, brainstone*); rhythms like shattering glass; breath-pauses presented on the page through a system of indentation he has apparently invented. The music can be as dense as the later Bunting; the language as personal as that of David Jones (though unlike Jones, Griffin never displays his erudition; the poems are entirely without literary reference). "The syntax," George Oppen has commented, "moves of its own force, moves in the force of the world, it restores light and space to poetry. It is what the poetry of England has lacked for— how long?"

He was first published in his (and the century's) fifties, and the work contains none of the indulgences of younger poets. There is wit but never cleverness, no fanciful speculation, no anecdote, few occasional pieces, and— other than some recent meditations on death— no autobiography, no confession. The "I" of the poem, when it appears, is linked only to verbs of thought, declaration or perception. Griffin's nuclear words are *man, God, music, pride, humility*. There is always the sense that the poet has been impelled to speech.

This may be the first poetry to contemplate seriously the new vision of earth given us by the lunar missions. It is a poetry of planetary consciousness, but without the occultism and nostalgia for a Golden Age that has characterized more popular writing. Accordingly, given the times, the vision is double; the poet's response both ecstasy and rage. The intense lyrics in celebration of natural beauty are almost eclipsed by the bleak and apocalyptic meditations. Griffin is one of the few poets today who is confronting, in the poem, this earth of pesticide, radiation, holocaust, overpopulation, deforestation, chemical waste— the way we live now, in the first age to devastate the future. His is a voice at world's end: "We need no prophets We know what is coming/ but can we live with it?"

Although the poems continue the English spiritual tradition (and indeed Griffin seems closer to Vaughan, Herbert and Traherne, Hopkins and Dixon, than to any poet of this century) the God of organized religion never enters these contemplations. Griffin's God is idiosyncratic and complex: a divine force which is either destructive or does not exist; a God that is the Goddess, planet earth; a God that "is men making music." One of his darkest lines simply states: "Entropy is God."

In the absence of a creator God, the poetry becomes spiritual in the broadest sense: the spirit of incantation— incantation meaning music, poetry, prayer ("I believe in prayer not in God.") In a world where "we voted with our feet a deadness to live in," Griffin's prayer is a grim one: "for/ Earth to be saved from Man." He writes: "I believe in man but not much."

Two thousand years ago, Wei Hung stated: "The music of an age on the verge of ruin is mournful and thoughtful." Griffin's music is both, and yet, given his vision, strangely ecstatic. For Jonathan Griffin, the "fact of music"— that it is there, that we are capable of making it— may be, in the end, all that matters:

Is it too late? Before it is too late
remember the great music. Because small
mammals dreamed it, because it is at all,
preserve the world, continue Man. Let great
work, by the few unlikely, inseminate
silence— the private silences, the All
Silence— with new music: to the still, small
tune of Man the last waste reverberate.

NOTES FOR *SULFUR* I

[Notes, *reviews, comments and responses written*
for the back pages of Sulfur, 1981-1986.]

....

Seidel's *Sunrise*

So what's a guy like me doing with a book like that in a place like this?

Well... Frederick Seidel is our latest most important American poet. *Sunrise*, seventeen years in the making, smartly published by Penguin/ Viking, is the 1979 Lamont Poetry Selection and the winner of the 1980 National Book Critics Circle Award (now second in prestige to the Pulitzer). Robert Lowell wrote in 1965: "When I read him, I have envious, delighted, jolted feelings and suspect the possibilities of modern poetry have been changed." Richard Poirier compares Seidel to Lawrence, calling *Sunrise* one of the best poetry books of the last decade or more. Jerome Mazzaro in the *Hudson Review* reveals that "Seidel has the power to be an important visionary." And Denis Donaghue, moonstruck in the *N.Y. Review of Books*, is reminded of— needless to say—

Yeats and Lowell. In other words, it is likely that few, if any, *Sulfur* subscribers have read the man.

One effect of the poetry pandemic has surely been the elimination of exogamous reading. It has become so hectic in one's own longhouse that one rarely has the time or stamina for visits to the other clans. Twenty years ago, in the ardent days of the anthology battles, even diehard Beat or Black Mountain partisans could, at the least, recognize the insignia of the opposing troops (double initials always made an easy target). Today, who among *Sulfur* readers (which I take as the progressive, but not radical, flank) can spot the ear of Alfred Corn, or distinguish between Howard and Stanley Mosses? Who among us doesn't think that a "line of Dubie's" refers to Frank Sinatra?

I, for one, read contemporary American poetry every day, receive a pile of poetry books and periodicals every week, yet rarely open any book of poetry published by a major house or as part of a university press poetry series (excepting selected/collected editions of the old or dead), any poetry book that wins a major prize, or any literary periodical with the word "Review" in the title. (Nor, I hasten to add, do I exclusively linger in that church bake-sale ozone where all the presses are named after exotic flora or common fauna.) Consequently, I am not only ignorant of 80% of the poets discussed at the moment by scholars, wits and literati; I am utterly mystified by the mechanics of current "establishment" taste— the grounds, say, for the inclusion or exclusion of any poem in or from any Review. This despite the fact— which we never admit— that on the whole the academic reviewers and critics are far better writers and far more informed than the average fellow traveler of those who make it new.

And so adrift with my nearly blank map of American poetry, I happened to read a review of Seidel's *Sunrise* by Vernon Young in the N.Y. *Times Book Review*. Seidel was unknown to me, but I recognized Young as a "frequent critic." Although, to remain calm, the *Book Review* is best avoided— one always makes the mistake of confusing it with literature, simply because it happens to deal with objects identical to those in which literature is traditionally stored— Young's piece caught my eye. Seidel's poems, he wrote, "were the best about hell written in this country"; urbane, scathing, frenetic"; "his visionary glimpses are balefully superb"; "compelling"; and so on. In support, he produced two passages from the book. The first, about Osip Mandelstam:

> *He was last seen alive*
> *In 1938 at a transit camp near Vladivostok*
> *Eating from a garbage pile,*
> *When I was two, and Robert Lowell was twenty-one,*
> *Who much later would translate Mandelstam,*
> *And now has been dead two years himself.*

And the second:

> *Antonioni walks in the desert shooting*
> Zabriskie Point. *He does not perspire*
> *Because it is dry. His twill trousers stay pressed,*
> *He wears desert boots and a viewfinder,*
> *He has a profile he could shave with, sharp*
> *And meek, like the eyesight of the deaf,*
> *With which he is trying to find America.*

These two excerpts struck me as not merely dull, but so spectacularly bad that I wondered what aesthetic could prize (literally, as it turned out) such work? What boat had I missed? I bought the book.

Seidel in *Sulfur* should, in fairness, be presented, not described— it's all too easy to sniff in dismissal or lower the heavy artillery, So instead of sitting duck, I offer "Pressed Duck," a poem in its entirety from the collection:

Caneton à la presse *at the now extinct Café Chauveron.*
Chauveron himself cooking, fussed
And approved
Behind Elaine, whose party it was;
Whose own restaurant would be famous soon.

Poised and hard, but dreaming and innocent—
Like the last Romanovs— spring buds at thirty, at thirty-two,
We were green as grapes,
A cluster of February birthdays,
All "Elaine's" regulars.

Donald, Elaine's then-partner,
His then-wife, a lovely girl; Johnny
Greco, Richardson, Elaine, my former wife, myself:
With one exception, born within a few days and years
Of one another.

Not too long before, thirty had been old,
But we were young— still slender, with one exception,
Heads and necks delicate
As a sea horse,
Elegant and guileless

Above our English clothes
And Cartier watches, which ten years later shopgirls
And Bloomingdale's fairies would wear,
And the people who pronounce chic *chick.*
Chauveron cut

The wine-red meat off the carcasses.
His duck press was the only one in New York.
He stirred brandy into the blood
While we watched. Elaine said,
  "Why do we need anybody else?
We're the world."

[Readers who do not happen to live on the island of Manhattan south of 96th Street will undoubtedly require some annotation. Elaine is the proprietor of Elaine's, a restaurant patronized by wealthy demi-intellectuals ("anti-Establishment" Hollywood directors, authors of "serious" bestsellers, et al). Elaine herself is well known both for her extreme snobbishness and her corpulence (i.e., the "one exception"). Cartier is, of course, one of the world's most elegant jewellers; Bloomingdale's, outwardly a department store, should be considered the Main Temple of the local consumer cult. A few years ago pressed duck became the rage, following a full-page article in the N.Y. *Times*; there was a run on duck-pressers at $500 apiece. One of the functions of the poem is to inform us that the poet was there first. It should also be noted that stanza 5 is not only snide, it is inaccurate: no shopgirl could possibly afford a Cartier watch, and no one on the island in recent memory has been heard to mispronounce a word which, in frequency of local usage, is second only to the first person pronoun (possessive case).]

Kindly souls might suspect that "Pressed Duck" is supposed to be funny, or ironic. It is not. He means it. For "Pressed Duck" is surrounded by thirty other poems of similar ilk, in a book dedicated to Bernardo Bertolucci: poems about partying with the Kennedys and Francis Bacon and Antonioni and apparently famous race car drivers; images of opium by the pool, Courrèges boots, *cuisine minceur*, Mercedes limos, skin-tight leather, handmade suits, Dom Perignon and Polaroid and Valium and Mao. There is a poem called "Fucking"; poems that end with one-line stanzas like "Goodbye." or "That is the poem."; and lines like "That is as sensitive as the future gets." or "Between his name and néant are his eyes." or "There and beyond one like heaven, as Che is."

When Seidel is trying to be funny, he sounds like this (the poem is about the author):

He sucked his pipe. He skied he fished he published.
He fucked his wife's friends. Touching himself he murmured
He was not fit to touch his wife's hem.
He dreamed of running away with his sister-in-law!
Of doing a screenplay. Him the guest on a talk show—

When he is serious, like this (on Robert Kennedy):

Younger brother of a murdered president,
Senator and candidate for president;
Shy, compassionate and fierce
Like a figure out of Yeats;
The only politician I have loved...

And mainly like this:

31

It was Union Square. I remember. Turn a corner
And in a light year
She'd have arrived
At the nearby inky, thinky offices of Partisan Review.
Was she off to see my rival Lief,
Boyfriend of girls and men, who cruised
In a Rolls convertible?

This is news that doesn't stay news with a vengeance: the invention of disposable poetry. It may be the least numinous poetry ever written, the poetry of a millisecond in an accelerating historical time, a poetry obsessed with dates and the ages of individuals, with the objects of fashion which the poet accepts literally and absolutely.

As such, the poetry has appeal to the bicoastal upper-middle brow— that is, people in Los Angeles who read *The New Yorker.* (Even the book itself is designed to look tony on a table in a high-tech interior.) Small wonder that book reviewers, whose words live less than a day, love it. But why is Academia bathed in the light of *Sunrise*? Why would a man like Donaghue mistake "Pressed Duck" for "Leda and the Swan"?

First, the book is not only not campy (which might have saved it), it is deeply humorless, therefore serious. Second, Seidel's stylistic models are clearly Lowell and, especially in the 14-page incomprehensible (Young: "enigmatic") title poem, Ashbery. What *Sunrise* offers, then, is some easily recognized gossip and glitz couched in the current academic mode. In short, perfect Leisure Reading for the English Department, or down at the inky thinky *Partisan Review*. Brancusi called Wagner's music a beefsteak in delirium; Seidel's poetry is a quiche on quaaludes.

Back at the dinky but kinky Sulfur, all I can do is nod as the sunrise sets.

[1981]

....

From S. Juan de la Cruz to St. John of the Cross

It is a curiosity that translation— the most passive, bookish act of writing— often occurs in a fit of anger. Appalled at the injustice of an existing translation, one rises in defense of the poem. Many translators have begun their careers out of rage at a perceived "betrayal" of a beloved text, and thus the worst translators have often turned out to be inadvertent forces of good. All of us who translate Spanish, for example, are forever indebted to Ben Belitt.

In the case of this poem by S. Juan de la Cruz (1542-1591), coincidental references to the text in manuscripts by Karin Lessing and Octavio Paz propelled me to check the translations I had at hand: Willis Barnstone's version, now in its sixth printing as a New Directions paperback; John Frederick Nims' recent third revision as a University of Chicago paperback; and Roy Campbell's translation, long out of print.
I found:

> *Aquella eterna fonte esta ascondida,*
> *que bien se yo do tiene su manida,*
> *aunque es de noche.*

33

literal: *That eternal fountain is hidden,*
                how well I know where it/ she has its/ her abode/
                   lair/ mansion,
                although it is night.

Nims: *Waters that flow forever and a day*
                through a lost country— oh I know the way
                in dark of night.

Barnstone: *The eternal fountain is unseen.*
                How well I know where she has been
                in black of night.

Campbell: *Its deathless spring is hidden, even so*
                Full well I guess from whence its sources flow
                Though it be night.

Nims had translated three words of the original, I know and night, and then simply made up the rest. Barnstone and Campbell seemed willing to do almost anything to complete a rhyme: Barnstone by stretching meaning (unseen for hidden, has been for has its/her lair— and even in Tin Pan Alley they don't rhyme unseen and has been) and Campbell by inventing sources flow and the convoluted and (oxy)moronic Even so/ full well I guess. Here was more:

                Su claridad nunca es escurecida,
                y se que toda la luz de ella es venida,

literal: *Its/her clarity is never darkened,*
                and I know that all light comes from her,

Nims: *A stream so clear, and never clouded? Never.*
                The wellspring of all splendor whatsoever.

Barnstone: *Her shining never has a blur;*
                I know that all light comes from her

Campbell: *Its clarity unclouded still shall be:*
                Out of it comes the light by which we see

                Aqui se esta llamando a las criaturas,
                y de esta agua se hartan aunque a escuras,
                porque es de noche.

literal: *Here it/she is calling to the creatures,*
                and with this water they are sated, although in
                  darkness,
                for it is night.

Nims: *Song of the waters calling: come and drink.*
                Come, all you creatures, to the shadowy brink
                in dark of night.

Barnstone: *She calls on all mankind to start*
                to drink her water, though in dark,
                for black is night.

Campbell: *Here to all creatures it is crying, hark!*
                That they should drink their fill though in the
                  dark,
                For it is night.

35

The patterns had remained the same throughout each version. Nims was simply out to lunch. (James Dickey, on the back cover, had hit the nailon the head: "You tend to forget that the poems were ever written in Spanish.") Barnstone and Campbell had collapsed from strenuous ministrations to that exacting god, rhyme: Campbell, like an old couch, showing great tufts of stuffing (*still shall be, by which we see, hark!*); Barnstone falling into a kind of baby-talk which he had mistaken for colloquial speech (*never has a blur, start/ to drink*).

My own version, a quick draft, was written, then, merely to give N. American readers some small sense of what S. Juan was talking about. It follows along the wide road cleared by Paul Blackburn's *Proensa*, where an attention to literal detail evolves a musical complex unlike that of the original. In attempting an exactitude of meaning— not at all difficult, given the poet's extraordinarily simple, limpid speech— I found it harmful either to keep the meter running or to retain the three-line stanzas of Juan's unorthodox *villancico*. This may distress those wardens who would prefer to keep the translation in a prosodic equivalent of the prison where the poem was originally written. But the point is that translation, especially translation of the classics, should have limitless possibility, no walls at all:

....

The Fountain

Although it is night
So well I know her
Fountain mounting
                    spilling out
  That eternal fountain
                              hidden
So well I know where
She keeps her lair
Though it is night

Although it is night
I will never know
                    her origin
She has no origin
And I know all origin comes from her
And I know there can be nothing more beautiful
That heavens, the earth drink from her
Though it is night

Although it is night
Her depth cannot be sounded
Well I know
                    no one may round her
And her clarity never darkens
And all light I know comes from her
Though it is night

Although it is night
I know her streams so abundant
Watering hells and heavens and man
The stream born from this fountain
Well I know so able
                        all-powerful
Though it is night

Although it is night
The stream of these two flows
Neither before the other goes
                        I know
This eternal fountain
                hidden
In this living bread to give us life
Though it is night

Here she calls to the creatures
And with this water they are slaked
Although in darkness for it is night

This the living fountain I desire
In this bread of life I see her
Though night

[1982]

....

A Case of AIDS Hysteria

[*Written in 1983, when* AIDS *was considered to be a disease affecting only gay men. Curiously, the* Rolling Stock *"award" may well have been the first mention of* AIDS *in the poetry press, and this the second.*]

*R*olling Stock is a cultural newspaper edited by Ed and Jennifer Dorn and published from the University of Colorado. Its latest issue, "numero 5," devotes a full page— written, I gather, in collaboration with Tom Clark— to the "1983 AIDS AWARDS FOR POETRY— In recognition of the current EPIDEMIC OF IDIOCY on the poetry scene." The page features a large illustration of a test-tube of reddish liquid, presumably infected blood: the "prize." At the bottom of the page is a photograph of two Asian men in suits wearing Mickey Mouse caps. The caption reads: "To date 1300 cases of AIDS POETRY have been reported in the U.S."

The recipients of this honor are Dennis Cooper ("for writing the most AIDS-like line of the year: 'Mark's anus is wrinkled, pink, and simplistically rendered, but cute'"); Clayton Eshleman (for "attacking a dead— and thus harmless— poet, Elizabeth Bishop," in a review in the *L.A. Times*); Robert Creeley (for writing extravagant blurbs for books by Stephen Rodefer and Joanne Kyger); Steve Abbott ("for accusing everybody who doesn't like him or his poetry of 'rabid homophobia'"); Allen Ginsberg (for claiming that he wrote some lyrics for the rock group The Clash

39

when supposedly he hadn't); and finally, "*WRITE-IN* CANDIDATE" ("Fill in the name of your favorite *POETRY IDIOT* here")

As "idiocy" goes— even poetry "idiocy"— these strike me as rather obscure misdemeanors. Cooper's line is hardly worth singling out (but in what way is it "AIDS-like? because it is homoerotic?); the Ginsberg is strictly a "so what" item; and the Abbott clearly the product of a personal grudge. Creeley's liking for Rodefer and Kyger and Eshleman's dislike of Bishop are scarcely cause for alarm. (In fact, I'm more alarmed that Dorn and Clark, of all people, feel that Bishop, of all people, needs protection from the barbarians trampling on her grave.)

The presenting of awards to "idiots" has always been a favored pastime for sophomoric wits. Luckily the sophomoric wits of poetry usually find other things to do, like writing grants proposals. Here, however, *Rolling Stock* is merely picking up where Robert Bly's *Fifties/Sixties/Seventies* left off. But Dorn and Clark have considerably raised the stakes from Bly's "Blue Toad," or whatever it was: For these supposed infractions of good taste, they not only wish the poets dead, but dead after a long and particularly gruesome disease.

It's not at all funny. And *Rolling Stock's* choice of AIDS as the vehicle of death is positively sinister. It has only one reading: if AIDS is "idiocy," then clearly the "idiots" are AIDS-victims— that is, gay men. For Cooper, Ginsberg and Abbott, who are publicly known as homosexual, it means: Those faggots should drop dead. For Creeley and Eshleman, publicly known as heterosexual, it means: They're idiots, therefore faggots, therefore they should drop dead from faggot disease. (And as for Asians in Mickey Mouse caps— presumably more "idiotic" than whites in similar attire— they can drop dead too.)

40

Sickening and pointless, its utter irrelevancy makes the matter barely worth mentioning. But admirers of Dorn, who are many, and of Clark, who are some, now face the task of recovering the poetry from the macho slobber. Most depressing is that these poets, like a village on the fringe of the Empire, can only reduce the news, when it reaches them, to family squabbles. Meanwhile people are dropping dead from AIDS, and its discovery has unleashed a wave of homophobia, both verbal and active. Worse, it has become the right-wing's counter to the left's categorization of cancer as the moral disease of the age. If cancer, as various liberationists have proclaimed, is the body's response to passion unnaturally repressed by society or personality, then AIDS, according to the right, is the result of unnatural passion: homosexuality itself, or promiscuous, "depersonalized" homosexuality.

There is no doubt that AIDS is widely seen— even by some of its victims— as the wrath of God. This mythologizing of disease not only erects enormous barriers to treatment and potential cure, but it also promotes a climate of fear that extends far beyond AIDS itself. Hell becomes other people: the "idiots" among us, out not only to physically destroy us, but to destroy our family structure, our "American" values. The current AIDS hysteria is merely an exaggerated and particularly shameless form of the continuing national dementias of racism and anticommunism.

Rolling Stock demonstrates how easily the objects of fear and hatred become jumbled: homosexuals, AIDS-victims, Asians, authors of book-jacket blurbs—"idiots" all. I once would have thought Dorn and Clark to be unlikely mouthpieces for Reagan America.

[*Postscript:* Steve Abbott died of AIDS in 1994.]

41

Mircea Eliade (1907-1986)

His earliest memory was crawling in the forest, having wandered away from his mother, and suddenly coming face to face with a resplendent blue lizard.

His earliest story, written as a child, began: "I met God at the end of a path. He had pulled a branch off a hazel tree and was trying to make a switch of it. 'You wouldn't have a penknife, by any chance?' he asked me." (The gods, from the beginning, needed his help.)

He trained himself to sleep only four hours a night. He learned Italian, French, Portuguese, English, Greek, Latin, Hebrew, Persian, Russian, Sanskrit, Bengali. As a teenager he published two novels and hundreds of shorter pieces: stories, accounts of his extensive walking trips through the countryside, literary criticism, essays on entomology, alchemy, Orientalism, religion. Like many others who would form the Bollingen group, he was attracted to Fascism by its glorification of an indigenous folk.

At 21 he went to India for three years. He studied Sanskrit twelve hours a day, had a doomed love affair (recounted in his novel *Bengali Nights*), and ended up as a yogi in a cave above Rishikesh. That conjunction— scholarship, sensuality, sacrality— describes his life.

By 30 he had written seventeen books in Rumanian: best-selling novels, collections of stories and essays, books on India, alchemy, oceanography, Babylonian cosmography. He had translated two volumes of T.E. Lawrence, and written his first book on Yoga in French. (A year later, his first book written in English.)

Because of the great books on Yoga and shamanism, and *Patterns in Comparative Religion; The Myth of the Eternal Return; Rites and Symbols of Initiation; The Forge and the Crucible; The Quest; The Sacred and the Profane; The Two and the One; Images and Symbols; Myths, Dreams and Mysteries;* the anthology *From Primitives to Zen;* the three-volume *A History of Religious Ideas;* he was (and is) the preeminent guide and encyclopedia to the manifestations of the ancient mysteries— for the second half of the century, our Frazer. "We are 'condemned,'" he wrote, "to learn and to reawaken to the life of the spirit through books."

And yet he considered his work as an historian of religion as ancillary to his fiction. His masterpiece, he thought, was the long novel *The Forbidden Forest.* [I had tried to read it, and gave up after a hundred pages. Years later, reading his journals, I came across this passage: "*Fôret Interdit.* Why do so many readers stop, discouraged, after a hundred pages?" If only they would realize that those pages are deliberately "confused, wordy, and awkward"— a "camouflage" for what is to come. Past those pages, "any intelligent reader would be captivated, obsessed."]

His friends were Bachelard, Jung, Bataille, Breton, Ionesco, Ortega y Gasset, Dumézil, Cioran. His death elicited only a few paragraphs in our "newspaper of record."

Eliade wrote "I arrived at cosmic sacralities by reflecting on the daily experiences of Rumanian or Bengali peasants." Never much of a theoretician, his subject was the "concrete spiritual life as it takes place in culture"— the stuff of the sacred. He was a man who read everything and remembered everything: any thing reminded him of everything else. For Eliade, to find God one could begin anywhere. He was, at heart, a Hindu— and often could barely disguise his impatience with the exclusionary policies of the three monotheisms. And he was— in his histories of religion perhaps more than in his fiction— a poet: one of the century's great celebrants of the ideas in things.

[1986]

....

GENUINE FAKES

[*Originally written as a review of Denis Dutton ed.,*
The Forger's Art *(University of California Press) for* The L.A. Weekly, *1983.*
Rewritten for an issue of Artes de México *devoted to forgeries, 1995.*]

About ten years after it was published, an energetic young man retyped Jerzy Kosinski's 1965 prize-winning novel, *The Painted Bird*, gave the manuscript a new title, and submitted it to a dozen American publishers. None of them, including Kosinski's own publisher, recognized the book, and all of them rejected it.

It was a good joke, and a telling comment on how books get published, but the story does not end there. Some years before Kosinski's death, an investigative journalist wrote an article claiming that the Polish author could not possibly have written *The Painted Bird* in English: at the time, he was a recent immigrant to the United States, and his command of the language was poor. It was suggested that he either wrote the novel in Polish and had it translated, or he outlined the story to an assistant who actually "wrote" the book. Either way, the book's acclaimed verbal pyrotechnics would not be the work of Kosinski. Furthermore, there were rumors that the novel was based on— or possibly plagiarized from— the writings of an unpublished Polish writer who had died in a concentration camp, and whose manuscript had somehow fallen into Kosinski's possession.

The Painted Bird is a classic case of how authorship determines reception. The memoir of a small boy in war-torn Poland, it would have been enveloped in unbearable pathos if it had been presented as the work of the murdered Pole. As it is, although the text remains the same, its importance diminishes, in the following order, according to the identity of its author: Kosinski as original writer, the translator, the assistant, Kosinski as plagiarist, the young re-typist. As Salvador Dali said, the first person to compare a woman's cheeks to a rose was undoubtedly a genius; the second person to do so could easily have been an idiot.

Forgery is the little pin that pricks the hot-air balloon of theories of art. Intellectually, we may believe, with the modernists, that in art all ages are contemporaneous— that a lyric by Sappho has the immediacy of a poem written yesterday— or believe, with the postmodernists, that there is no author, only the text. But the actual reading or looking or listening to a work of art always occurs in the tension between our perception of the work itself and our knowledge of its origin. Even when the author is Anonymous (as the old joke goes, the greatest writer who ever lived) the work is inextricably placed in its historic moment. Its timelessness is its unchanging core, which keeps the work alive over the centuries. Its location in time— moreover in a time that is receding— keeps the work in constant flux. We see the work as part of an archaic context, a context we must enter into, but we see it with modern eyes— that is, with the eyes of a modernity that is always changing.

A forgery is an object without a creator, and human nature cannot bear anything without a narrative of its origin. (The liveliest debate in physics today is the question that every age and culture has had to answer: what happened in the first four seconds of the universe?) There is no reason why an exact copy (assuming it were possible) of a painting should be inferior to the original, but we *know*, emotionally if not rationally, that it is so. Mark Twain said that Wagner's music was better than it sounds. A forgery is always worse than it looks.

Forgery is based on authenticity, and both of them are jokes. But it is authenticity, not forgery, that is the cruelest joke of all. The Metropolitan Museum buys a Greek vase for a million dollars that is hailed as the masterpiece of its kind, until it is revealed as a fake. We venerate da Vinci's "Last Supper," even though it has been restored so many times it no longer has any of its original paint. We ponder the quite serious critical proposal that the plays of Shakespeare were not written by William Shakespeare, but by another man of the same name. Yesterday's attribution to the hand of the Master becomes today's relegation to an anonymous "From the studio of..." Nothing is more certain than the foolishness of old certainties.

But if authenticity leaves a taste of bitter regret, forgery at its best is a sugared hilarity. When it is done for monetary gain it is as humorless as a counterfeit bill: all skill and no wit. When it is a work of megalomania it is at its most perverse, the combination of skill and obsession that leads to the pleasure of seeing one's efforts hanging in a museum or sold at Sotheby's. But the perversity of the humor is that it can never be shared: the forger must laugh alone. Forgery is at its most comic when it is an act of simple revenge, and when that act is, in the end, revealed.

For example, the pianist Alexis Weissenberg was tired of reading reviews that claimed he was a "cold, unemotional" performer. So he invented— what else?—a soundless piano. He then gave a concert where he played a tape recording of himself, and accompanied the music with precisely coordinated histrionic gestures and passionate grimaces. The hoax was not discovered, and the critics hailed the evening as one of Weissenberg's most moving performances.

An elaborate combination of revenge and megalomania, and one with more serious consequences, was the case of the century's greatest (known) forger, Hans van Meegeren. Born in Holland in 1889, he had some success as a very young artist, most notably for a drawing of Queen Juliana's pet deer, which still appears on Dutch Christmas cards. But the utterly dreadful Symbolist canvasses he began painting in his late twenties were receiving the kind of reviews usually reserved for misunderstood genius or well-understood mediocrity. Needing money, he made his first forays into the forging business by producing fakes of Frans Hals, Ter Borch, and de Hoogh. They sold moderately well. He then discovered his true mission in life, the master plan:

Vermeer had recently been rediscovered, and was rightly being celebrated as a rival to Rembrandt as the avatar of Dutch genius. There was, however, a large chronological gap in Vermeer's thirty-odd known works: his early years when, it was thought, he had travelled to Italy, fallen under the influence of Caravaggio, and painted works with religious themes— unlike his later landscapes, interiors, and portraits. As it happened, the art critics who were indulged in speculating on Vermeer's missing paintings were the very same who had consigned van Meegeren to the Siberia of modern taste.

It was perfect. Van Meegeren went into seclusion in France and, after years of perfecting the preparation of materials that would delude scientific examination— to this day some of his techniques cannot be explained— he proceeded to produce the missing

Vermeers. His greatest work, "The Supper at Emmaus," was declared by one critic— a particular enemy of van Meegeren— to be not only authentic, but "*the* masterpiece of Vermeer." The painting was sold in 1937 for the equivalent of 1.4 million dollars, and it hung, to great adulation, in the Boysman Museum for seven years.

It would, perhaps, still be there were it not for the inevitable twist of fate. After the Second World War, it was discovered that van Meegeren had sold a Vermeer to Hermann Göring. He was arrested for stealing a Dutch National Treasure and selling it to the enemy. To escape a conviction of treason, van Meegeren was forced to confess that the painting was a fake— and moreover, that all the newly-found Vermeers were van Meegerens. He was not believed, and the police insisted he produce a Vermeer in prison, which he did. Yet despite his confession and conviction for forgery— he died in prison soon after— there were some critics who stubbornly maintained that "The Supper of Emmaus" was indeed a genuine Vermeer that the forger was claiming as his own. They successfully pleaded with the Dutch government not to destroy the painting, in case a mistake had been made.(The argument, curiously, against capital punishment.) Finally, in an odd reversal, the pop novelist Irving Wallace published an article in 1947 celebrating van Meegeren as a hero who had swindled Göring. (We now know that van Meegeren was a Nazi sympathizer who had no choice when Göring asked for the painting.)

Looking at "The Supper of Emmaus" today, it seems incredible that this unspeakably clumsy canvas was ever mistaken for the real thing. As an authentic Vermeer, it is pathetic. But as an original van Meegeren it is a brilliant parody which, in one startling gesture, both delivers the last laugh and anticipates postmodern ironic/ iconic pastiche: van Meegeren clearly copied the face of Jesus from a photograph of Greta Garbo.

Forge: the same word for falsifying artworks and shaping metal by heating and hammering. In traditional societies, the black-smith, the maker of the weapons, is, like the shaman, a source of great power who is kept apart from the rest of the community through a web of taboos. In our society, it is the forger who has taken the Romantic ideals of the isolation of the artist to its great-est extreme. He is a maker of art who can never be acknowledged as such, whose work is acclaimed while he remains in total anonymity. He is an outcast from the outcasts of society. And yet, he is also the purest artist: the one who rejects the cult of person-ality, who has no identity and no personal style, who believes only in the work itself and the age to which it is attributed. The forger, in the end, may be the model artist.

....

AN AVIARY OF TARNS

[*Written as the entry on Nathaniel Tarn for the reference book,*
Contemporary Poets *(St. Martin's), 1984.*]

I remember on the shores of the most beautiful lake in the
  world
whose name in its own language means abundance of waters
as if the volcanoes surrounding it had broken open the earth
there in the village of Saint James of Compostela one cold night
not the cereus-scented summer nights in which a voice I never
  traced
sang those heartbreaking serenades to no one known
a visiting couple gave birth in the market place
the father gnawing the cord like a rat to free the child
and before leaving in the morning they were given the
  freedom of the place
                    I mean the child was given

A child of nowhere, Nathaniel
Tarn has been given, and has given himself, a freedom of place
that is rare among contemporary poets. Anglo-French by birth, a

dual citizen, his childhood was bilingual, and he was educated on both sides of the Channel. In the 1950's and 1960's he had a short career as a (self-described) "25th-rate" French Surrealist poet, and a more successful run as an up-and-coming young English poet: an associate of the literary group called "The Group," and editor of the extraordinary Cape Editions. Furthermore, he was an anthropologist, a student of Lévi-Strauss and Griaule in Paris and Redfield in Chicago, writing monographs on the Atitlán region of Guatemala. And he was a Buddhist scholar, author of, among other writings, a book on the monastic politics of Burma. In 1970 Tarn followed his literary affinities and moved to the United States where, at the moment— always subject to sudden metamorphosis— he is an American poet and citizen, a professor of comparative literature, and a Mayanist. As an anthropologist he continues to write on Guatemala, and as a Buddhist scholar he is involved with the Tibetan diaspora. Much of his writing, particularly the prose, has appeared under other names.

This range of Tarns is mirrored, in his four major book-length poems, in a poetry of place where the place is always changing (*The Beautiful Contradictions*); a love poetry where the object of desire undergoes countless transformations (*Lyrics for the Bride of God*); and a deeply personal poetry which the poet allows to be spoken by others (*A Nowhere for Vallejo*, which is a collage of lines and invented lines by the Peruvian poet, in Spanish and English translation, mingled with the voice of "Tarn"); and *Alashka*, written with Janet Rodney, perhaps the century's only collaborative poem which does not identify the individual contributions. Moreover the poetry has, in the poet's words, frequent "unconscious thrusts, sudden irruptions into the body of the work, almost like spirit-cult possessions," where the poet speaks in other voices, and sometimes other languages.

What holds it together is Tarn's ecstatic vision, his continuing enthusiasm for the stuff of the world. It is a poetry whose native tongue is myth, and it rolls out in long lines of sacred hymns that oscillate between the demotic and the hieratic (heir to Smart and Blake, to Whitman and the Neruda of *The Heights of Macchu Picchu*, which he translated) and sequences of short poems, small linked bursts of sharp image and speech, which tie Tarn to Williams and contemporary practitioners like Snyder and Kelly.

Since the death of Kenneth Rexroth, he is, with Michael McClure, the major celebrant of heterosexual love in the language. His combination of ingenious metaphor and sexual exuberance has been rare in the language since the 17th century. (Indeed, much of Tarn's American work may be read as an epic elaboration of Donne's erotic geography of the "new found land.") Like Rexroth, he is the author of travel narratives that restore the adjective "readable" to poetry. And, like Rexroth and MacDiarmid, his poetry encompasses Eastern philosophy, world myth, revolutionary politics, and precise descriptions of the natural world. His poems have more birds than Clare's.

Not an exile, longing for the abandoned home, but a nomad, longing for the idea of home: it is the American condition, and the Jewish condition. Tarn, both American and Jewish, has declared that *sparagmos* ("the falling to pieces/ the tearing to pieces/ of the world as body") is "the inescapable theme of our time." (And he can, at times, be as indignant as Pound at the destroyers of culture and of the wilderness.) His poetry, along with that of few others these days, sets course for a mythical unity: the *hierosgamos*, marriage of earth and sky, when history will

be forever in the present tense, somewhere will be everywhere,
and the author everyone:

that the branch may break
that the long voyage may end for the planet
and the furthest point of death be returned from
the separation into dead and live
summer and winter, and only green be seen above
ground
that he might go home

BLACK MOUNTAIN

[*Originally written as a review of Mary Emma Harris,*
The Arts at Black Mountain College *(M.I.T. Press) for* The Nation, *1987.*
Rewritten for publication in Mexico, 1989.]

O nly in America could an art school be imagined as a form of Utopia, yet that is precisely how Black Mountain College (1933-1956) lingers in the memory. Set in a magnificent corner of the Blue Ridge Mountains, it was a community where students and teachers lived together, raised their own food, built their own dorms and classrooms, and jointly determined both their courses of study and the courses of their lives. It was an outpost of aestheticism through the Depression, two hot wars and the cold war, and it attracted an extraordinary collection of European refugees from fascism and American refugees from capitalism. It was the kind of place where Josef Albers determined the way the cans should be stacked in the kitchen, and where the evening's entertainment might be a play with music by John Cage and dances by Merce Cunningham, sets by Elaine and Willem de Kooning, costumes by Richard Lippold, direction by Arthur Penn, and Buckminster Fuller as the leading man.

Fuller built his first geodesic dome at Black Mountain, and Cage first played his silent music and staged the first "happening." Its resident artists (students and teachers) were Albers, the de Koonings, Rauschenberg, Kline, Lippold, Shahn, Feininger, Zadkine, Bolotowsky, Chamberlain, Noland, deCreeft, Twombly, Tworkov, Vicente, Greene. Gropius taught architecture; Cunningham, deMille, Humphrey and Litz taught dance. Its composers were Harrison, Wolpe, Sessions, Krenek; its photographers Callahan, Siskind, Newhall and Morgan. Radin taught anthropology; von Franz mythology, Rudofsky the history of costume. Paul Goodman was there, and Alfred Kazin, Clement Greenberg, Eric Bentley, Eric Kahler, Clark Foreman, Edward Dahlberg, M.C. Richards. And, in its last years, Charles Olson, Robert Creeley and Robert Duncan were the centrifugal forces of a poetics movement that came to be classified, however erroneously, as the Black Mountain school.

Although it was a short-lived and tiny institution— 1200 students in its 24 years, most of them in attendance only for a summer— Black Mountain existed in such a state of perpetual schism and flux that it defies any generalization of intents or purposes. There were, essentially, three Black Mountains, each in turn composed of idiosyncratic members who rarely agreed on very much. The first was the college founded in 1933 by John Andrew Rice and a group of renegade faculty and students from a Congregational Church college in Florida, and whose guiding light, until 1949, was Josef Albers. The second was the remarkable series of summer sessions that were held, with some interruptions, from 1944 to 1953. And the third was the small, mainly literary band of outsiders, led by Charles Olson, that more or less camped in the ruins of the college from 1951 to 1956.

Rice was an iconoclastic classicist who delighted in the *enfant terrible* role, and taught by questioning everything, particularly cherished beliefs. When he and his fellow exiles from Rollins College took over some Baptist Assembly buildings on Black Mountain in 1933, they came with few specific plans and one general ideal: to break down the institutionalization (and, for Rice, the "excessive feminization") of the American college. At Black Mountain, faculty and students were to be held jointly and equally responsible for every aspect of their lives and education. There was to be no "administration" and no outside governing body, such as trustees; decisions were to be made by the community as a whole, according to the Quaker "sense of the meeting." Grades and requirements were to be abolished; athletics would be replaced by useful work on the farm and in maintenance. Most important, art was to be the central force— not, as elsewhere, an extra-curricular activity— in the student's general education.

Into this hotbed of American progressivism came the coolest of the European modernists: Josef Albers, who had left Germany after the forced closing of the Bauhaus and had arrived in Buncombe County, North Carolina not speaking a word of English. ("All I knew was Buster Keaton and Henry Ford.") In a country without culture, but "hungry for a culture," he saw himself as a kind of cultural-spiritual adviser, leading students in a disciplined program of self-discovery through controlled experiments in the elements of form. "Abstracting," he wrote, "is the essential function of the Human Spirit." The rest was distraction.

This meant that no art history was taught at Black Mountain during the Albers years, and no one sketched or painted the exquisite landscape. Art was a series of problems to be solved: the interactions of shapes and colors (only colored paper was used, not variable paint), the split between the"physical" and "psychical" effects of matter. Thus the students labored to make the hard look soft, the wet dry, the warm cold. Wood was made to look like water, egg shells to look like flower petals, wire screen and leaves to look like shadows. Jewelry was made from paper clips and kitchen utensils; kernels of corn were meticulously arranged to give the appearance of a piece of woven cloth.

Albers— disciplined, opinionated, autocratic, "a beautiful teacher and an impossible person," according to Robert Rauschenberg— was to be the determinative force at Black Mountain for seventeen years. Nearly everything that happened there during the regular school year can be seen as a result of, or a reaction against, his presence. Against a succession of idealistic and younger faculty members, he stood his ground on the side of educational ideals vs. an ideal community, aesthetic preoccupation vs. social concerns, isolation vs. interaction with the rest of the world. (That these were seen as contradictory impulses may have been the school's undoing.)

Albers had no patience for "this constant over-democratic nonsense." He insisted that teachers know more about teaching than students, and gradually the students lost their equal role in the administration of the college. He had no interest in the farm, and deplored the sloppiness of the students' Bohemian dress. Certain crafts— weaving (taught by Anni Albers), woodworking, bookbinding— were permitted, but ceramics, for one, was verboten ("ashtray art"). Most important, Albers was relentlessly apolitical, and opposed to the teaching of the social sciences and history. Perhaps the most shocking aspect of Black Mountain during the Albers years is its studies obliviousness to the dramatic contemporary events. When the students performed a proletarian drama by Irwin Shaw, instead of the usual folk plays and Ibsen, Albers stormed out. Students would gather every Saturday to listen to the Texaco opera, but when, six months into World War II, a student brought a radio into the dining hall to hear the news, there was a general scandal. None of the histories of the college mention any interest in the Spanish Civil War.

Albers was also largely successful in isolating the community from what was imagined as "the outside world." This meant not only the opposition of other faculty members' proposals for social work in the community, voter registration drives, crafts programs and the like, but, more devastating, a continual purging of elements that were seen as adversely affecting the image of the college. There was a quota for Jews until the late 40's. Left-wingers— most notably Eric Bentley, Clark Foreman and Paul Radin— were forced out. Homosexuals were tolerated only if they kept their activities secret. And, in a long and particularly divisive battle, Albers and his followers kept Black Mountain segregated, despite overwhelming opposition by the students, until 1944, when one female black day student was allowed to take classes. (Only a few other blacks attended over the next five years.)

Year after year, during the fall, winter and spring, the tiny fiefdoms, each led by a charismatic faculty member, waged war for the ideological control of the community and the college. It was not until 1944, with the inauguration of special summer sessions that included many of the regular students and few of the faculty, that Black Mountain achieved the Utopian quality that sustains its reputation today.

It should be remembered that nearly all of the luminaries associated with Black Mountain attended only the summer sessions, and usually for a single summer. Many of them were young and penniless at the time. They were given a few months of vacation in the country— room and board but no pay— and the freedom to teach as much or as little as they pleased, and whatever they pleased. Meals were communal, and most of the teaching took place over a dining room table—"education as conversation," Cage called it. Those in the performing arts had an extraordinary opportunity to realize their work: an eager cast of student and faculty dancers, musicians, actors, as well as painters and sculptors to create the sets. Alliances formed or strengthened at Black Mountain— among Cage, Cunningham, Rauschenberg, Fuller, Harrison and Lippold, for example— would have lasting effects on the art of each.

Above all, there were too many stars for any one person to dominate, and none of them carried any vested interest in the community. The subject became the making of art, not the defining of an art school, and the flow of temporary visitors effectively prevented institutional petrification. Moreover, the provisional and improvisatory nature of the summer sessions rhymed perfectly with the techniques that were being explored at the time by Cage and the others: chance operations, random juxtaposition, the introduction of the accidental into the "finished" work, the mixing of media, the dismantling of the "art object." To have Cage on a ladder reading Meister Eckhart while Rauschenberg simultaneously played scratchy Piaf records on a wind-up Victrola, Cunningham danced through the audience chased by a barking dog, David Tudor hammered a prepared piano, and slides and movies were screened at odd angles on the wall, was the exact opposite of Albers' meticulous arrangements of given forms. For one Albersian at the Cage happening, it was "the Dark Ages."

Albers and the entire art faculty resigned in 1949, and that vision of the Dark Ages became the shadow cast by the gigantic Charles Olson, for whom "the poet [was] the only pedagogue left." The school, in many ways, became its opposite: writing was emphasized, rather than art; the largely female student body became predominantly male; the upbeat progressives of the 30's and 40's became the drunken nihilists of the 50's, exiles from the postwar materialist boom; politics became a matter of hot debate; "process" replaced "form" as the key word.

Olson envisioned Black Mountain as a "twin" to the Princeton Institute of Advanced Studies, and outlined grand schemes of visiting lecturers and consecutive series of long symposia on nearly every aspect of human knowledge ("a curriculum of the soul"). But he was no administrator, and in McCarthy's America the college was attracting more F.B.I. agents than students. The school fell apart. The dining room was closed, and the students fended for themselves. The farm was abandoned, its barn uncleaned, its cows sick and freezing to death. Kudzu vines overran the campus, and the classrooms were piled with trash. In the music library, the phonograph records had been melted down to look like Dali's painting. There was, in Olson's words, "no more of this community bullshit"; in fact there was hardly a community. In its last years, the school had less than twenty students and teachers; most of them professional (or would-be) artists more interested in their own work than in any educational or communal ideals.

And yet this tiny band of outsiders formed the only arts movement to which the name "Black Mountain" has been attached. Olson brought in Robert Creeley and Robert Duncan (who in 1938 had been expelled from the college, after one day, because of his homosexuality and anarchist views); and students such as Edward Dorn, Joel Oppenheimer and Jonathan Williams wandered in. Together they resurrected the American small press poetry scene with a flurry of publishing: pamphlets and broadsides on the school's own presses, Williams' Jargon Press, and

The Black Mountain Review, which under Creeley's direction became the best "little" magazine of the 1950's. By 1960, four years after the college had closed, Donald Allen's anthology *The New American Poetry* had formally christened the six poets (along with others who had never attended, such as Paul Blackburn, Larry Eigner and Denise Levertov) as the Black Mountain school.

As a movement the poets were largely united in their rejection of the contemporary New Criticism and its well-crafted poem-objects poured into the molds of traditional prosody. For Creeley, form was "never more than an extension of content"; for Duncan, the poem was an event: "not a record of an event, but the event itself"; for Olson, the poet's own breath was to determine the measure of the line; for Levertov, the poem was an organic entity. Most shared an allegiance to William Carlos Williams and a poetry written in a natural American speech; some believed, with Ezra Pound, that the subject of poetry was everything, that poetry was the best way to talk about everything. If the poems in the academic journals of the time were flotillas of small craft, Olson hoped to launch ships of state. He often compared himself and his handful of students with Mao in the caves of Yenan. As the North Carolina version of Black Mountain dwindled, Olson imagined a network of Black Mountain satellites and cells across the nation: a force.

It is curious that both Albers and Olson spent a great of deal of time in Mexico in the late 1940's and early 50's. Albers saw the pre-Columbian pyramids as expressions of a pure form which he could reduce to a few lines on a page. (And, in a weird bit of anthropological fantasy, declared that Black Mountain was "consciously on the side" of the "Mayan Indians who demanded that the King be the most cultivated among them.") Olson saw the hieroglyphs as poetry, perfect embodiments of the things they represented, and remarked on countless examples— from the domestication of corn to the way the Indians walked— of what he considered to be the Mexicans' seamless unification of intellect and physicality. In one of his most famous sentences he exclaimed, "O, they were hot for the world they lived in, these Maya, hot to get it down the way it was— the way it is, my fellow citizens."

Cold and hot, the winds that emanated from Black Mountain have never dissipated. There is a direct line of formalist preoccupation from Albers to the Abstract Expressionists to the Pop and Op painters to the conceptualists to the current breed of neo-Expressionists, neo-Geos and other quality merchants. Albers would be at home in a Museum of Modern Art that exhibits a Polynesian spirit fetish, drained of its religious and social context, next to a Giacometti because both are anthropomorphic, tall and thin. The cold has dominated the century; the hot remains the permanent heterodox. Olson never won a major prize (nor have Creeley or Duncan); he died with his work largely out of print. Today, of course, there is a shelf-full of critical studies, but the poets alive and working out of Olson's image of what poetry ought to be remain as marginal as Pound or Williams or Olson were in their own times.

At Black Mountain, both the Albers years and the Olson years were small triumphs amidst a larger disaster. It may, in the end, be impossible to create a community of artists in a secular society. And— though we assume the beneficence of ventures such as Black Mountain and its scores of spin-offs— perhaps it was a mistake to assume that the function of such a community should be education. The inseparable identification of art and school is

a recent development. In 1914, the proto-Dadaist poet and box-
er Arthur Cravan, raging against art schools, ended his diatribe
with this prophetic line: "I am astonished that some crook has
not had the idea of opening a writing school."

....

LOST WAX / FOUND OBJECTS

[*Written as the text to the catalog*, Bronze Ages: Brian Nissen's Sculpture,

(Clarion Press), 1987.]

....

"One creates an organism when the elements are ready for life."
Tristan Tzara

I

"Good sculpture," wrote Ezra Pound, thinking about Gaudier-Brzeska, "does not occur in a decadence. Literature may come out of a decadence, painting may come out of a decadence, but in a decadence men do not cut stone." Within that hyperbole— written, strangely, in spite of the evidence at hand: a master stonecutter killed in a pointless war— is a small seed of truth.

Decadence implies a self-absorbed present: one that may yearn for certain lost moments of history, but in which history has attenuated, and the ancient knowledge, beliefs, customs, mores have lost their vitality. Religion becomes superstition, custom entwines with commerce, taboo turns to common practice. That literature and painting are produced in ages of decadence may owe, in part, simply to their materials, which have so little history. To write (in the West) is to use the language, however stylized, of one's contemporaries— a language not much older than one's grandparents. One paints with materials that are only a few centuries or a few decades old: oil, watercolor, acrylic. But to sculpt— literally to "sculpt": carving or shaping stone, wood, clay, wax— is to work with one's hands on ancient matter: to remain in the present while simultaneously inserting oneself into a continuum that begins in the archaic.

To work in bronze is to immerse oneself in a process that has remained unchanged since its invention in Egypt in 2600 B.C. It is to create pieces that— no matter how new or idiosyncratic in form— share their molecules and the act of their making with Anatolian winged centaurs and bull's heads from Ur, Cretan double axes and Corinthian helmets, Saxon heads with silver eyes, Persian ewers incised with lovers and cuirasses with inscriptions from the Qu'ran, Etruscan sunburst oil lamps, hunting reliefs from Vace, Shang bells and drums and tall-stemmed bowls, the long-tailed birds of the Chou, their vessels covered with meanders and continuous volutes, their monster masks with ring handles, their animal-headed daggers and knives, cheekpieces, jingles, harness fittings, the mirrors inscribed "May we never forget each other" with which the Han nobility were buried, shields from Battersea and Celtic buckets, battle-axes from Luristan, Greek charioteers, kings of Nineveh, the gates of the Assyrian palace of Balawat, Marcus Aurelius on his horse, the doors of St. Sophia in Byzantium and St. Zeno in Verona, the seven-branched Easter candlesticks of Rheims, Gothic fonts and covers, Romanesque chandeliers and pelican lecterns, Parthian perfume stills, Moorish aquamanales in the shape of lions, the huge eyes and blank stares of Benin masks and heads, lanterns of musical Boddhisattvas from Nara, Bamun pipes of lizards and ancestors stacked like totem poles, the saints and miracles on the doors of Pisa, Renaissance lamps in the shape of a foot, in the shape of a man with his head between his legs (or worse),Donatello's plaquettes, Degas' dancers, Rodin's ponderer, filigreed flower baskets from Kamakura and the four-thousand-pound statue of Queen Napirassu of the Elam, three thousand years old and headless now, but with her hands delicately crossed... Objects created out of a marriage— traditionally celebrated as such— of copper and tin, whose officiant, the smith, was revered and reviled, subject to the same taboos as priests. Objects created in a process that has always been seen as a metaphor of the sacred mysteries: the wax is shaped and encased in clay, baked in a kiln until the clay hardens and the wax runs out, leaving the mold into which the bronze is poured. "Lost wax": only when there is nothing, when one has created a nothing, can the work be achieved.

"Sculpture," said Brancusi, "is not for young men."

II

To which, looking at Nissen's work, must be added another layer of history: the New World— which made knickknacks of bronze, but never had a Bronze Age— before the arrival of the Old.

Nissen, born in England in 1939, went to Mexico at age twenty-three and stayed for seventeen years, with frequent visits since. [And there too, a long line of British ancestors: Thomas Blake in Tenochtitlán only thirteen years after Cortés; Robert Tomson in 1556 accurately prophesying that one day it would be "the most populous Citie in the world"; that meticulous 18th century observer, Thomas Gage; Frederick Catherwood, discoverer and the great draughtsman of the Mayan ruins; the chronicler of 19th century drawing rooms, Frances Calderón de la Barca, a Scot married into Mexican society; the archeologist Alfred Maudslay; Henry Moore, appropriating the reclining figure of the Maya-Toltec *chac mool*; the Surrealist Leonora Carrington; Lawrence, Huxley, Waugh, Greene, Lowry; and the anonymous legions of scholars and bohemians, repressed voluptuaries, missionaries, drunks, xenophobes and aristocrats gone native— those who went to escape and those who went to find.]

Nissen, escaping the airless club room of post-imperial England, found in Mexico, as so many Europeans before him, vivacity— a vivacity that extends even into its obsession with death— and a unity, still extant in the hinterlands, of art and life. (Antonin Artaud: "In Mexico, since we are talking about Mexico, there is no art: things are made for use. And the world is in perpetual exaltation.") Above all, he found its indigenous history. Three of the forms of pre-Columbian expression are essential to Nissen's work: the glyph, the codex, and the temple. Their elaborations are tracks towards Nissen's work:

The Mayan glyphs are important here not for their individual meanings (decipherment) but for their system of construction. They were laid out on a grid that could be followed in a variety of directions. Within each rectangle of the grid, the individual glyph itself was a conglomerate of component parts (much like the Chinese ideogram): simple pictographs (a house for "house," a vulture for "vulture"), phonetic signs (each representinga single syllable), logographs (non-representational representations of a word), and semantic determinatives (specifiers of particular meaning).

For the Western mind— if not to its native practitioner— the glyph or the ideogram has a concreteness, a weight, that does not exist in alphabetic writing: the word is an object. Further, it seems— particularly to those who cannot "read" them— that each glyph, each word, has the *same* weight, that the glyphs are equal to one another, giving each thing in the world an identity of correspondence.

The extraordinary scholarship, and partial decipherment, that has occurred in recent years has proven that the glyphs are even more complex. The Mayaologist Linda Schele notes— to take one example— that the word "vulture" could be written in pictographic form, geometric form, or syllabic form. A pictographic vulture with a crown was one of the many ways of writing *ahau*, which meant both "lord" and one of the day-names of the Maya calendar. The pictographic vulture could also refer specifically to the black-headed vulture called *tahol* (literally, "shithead"). From that, the vulture glyphs (whether pictographic or geometric) were also used to represent *ta'* ("shit") or *ta* (a preposition meaning "to, on, from"). There were, then, nearly endless ways to write any given word, and Mayan scribes were valued for their punning and ability to coin new variations while strictly adhering to the rules.

This meant not only that each word was an *assembled object*, but that each object was in a state of perpetual metamorphosis, its meaning only comprehensible for the moment it is seen in the context of the other object-glyphs. That metamorphosis, within the larger repetitions of circular time, remains, in Mexico, a constant. In the poetry of the Aztecs, the poet becomes the poem itself, which becomes a plant growing within the poem; the plant becomes the fibers of the book in which the poem is painted; the fibers of the book become the woven fiber of the mat, the symbol of worldly power and authority. Octavio Paz's "Hymn Among the Ruins" ends with this famous line: "words that are flowers that are fruits that are acts."

Nissen, then, constructs his sculptures as glyphs. His work table is covered with small components fashioned out of wax: tiny balls, cylinders, zigzags, donuts, squares, cubes, lozenges, triangles, rods, j-shapes, pellets. In an interview, Nissen has commented: "I use a method based on the found object. The difference being that first, I make the objects, then I find them. Then I assemble them." He has remarked elsewhere that he also considers those components as parts of speech— given elements capable of a near-infinity of combinations. Their assembly is reminiscent, above all, of language as it is used by children, poets, punsters. The result— the individual piece of sculpture— is a phrase, a stanza (literally the "room" in which the words are arranged), a single moment of relation permanently frozen in bronze.

Nissen has also worked extensively, and with great originality, in the creation of codices. There were two kinds of Mexican codices, screen-fold books painted on both sides. The Mayan— of which only four survive— largely consisted of a hieroglyphic text accompanied by some illustration. The later codices are more extraordinary: Each page presented complex images— not all of them pictographic— that served as mnemonic devices for the priestly elite trained to "read" them, but were incomprehensible to outsiders. It is a kind of "text" unknown outside the New World, but which has its parallels in the geometric patterns of Amazonian baskets and Peruvian woven cloth, both of which could be "read." [Dennis Tedlock points out that the Maya word for the codex was *ilbal*, or "instrument for seeing." Today the word is used to refer to telescopes.]

Nissen has continued, in traditional screen-fold book form, the pictographic experiments on canvas of Klee, Tobey, Gottlieb, and Torres-García. His "Madero Codex" invents a witty language of jigsaw puzzle pieces, wooden matchsticks, cigarette butts, human figures (perhaps the Mayan "smoking gods"?), crossword puzzles, gridworks of letters that seem to, but don't quite, spell words like "glyph" and transform into a Mondrian "boogie-woogie." In its translation of traditional into contemporary imagery, it is reminiscent of the strangest illustrations in Mexican historiography: those that accompanied F.J. Clavijero's *Historia Antigua de México*, published in 1780. In that book the artist, rather than presenting the usual heavily stylized renderings of the Mexican originals, simply "interpreted" the glyphs and codices and redrew them in the current fashion. Thus, if he thought he saw, in the original, a hand holding a fish, he drew a hand holding a fish in the style of an 18th century lithograph. The elaborations are wonderful: a running figure with a daisy head, a man with a lily growing from his nose, a snake crowned with arrows. Clavijero's book, whose intentions were scientific, becomes, for us, Surrealism. Nissen, with no pretense of historical realism, creates both a science and a grammar.

Nissen's more complex "Itzpapalotl Codex" takes off from the Aztec goddess Obsidian Butterfly and a prose poem on the subject by Octavio Paz. It consists of grids of invented glyphs (some of whose components are recognizable small metal objects: keys, wrenches, nuts and bolts, horseshoe magnets, tuning forks, springs); electronic circuits; graffiti (*mosca*, fly; *tinieblas*, darkness; *Ramón, Pepe, Berta*...); butterflies; clippings and maps concerned with the village of Pápalotl, home of the goddess' shrine; encyclopedia entries on the goddess; Maya numbers; and so on. These represent, according to their author, a calendar, an entomological taxonomy, a topography, a mathematical reckoning (an accounting, in all the meanings of the word), auguries, and an inventory of tributes the goddess has received. The result is extraordinary: beautiful images that leave us just short of comprehension. Much like the ancient codices, in order to understand it the initiated (of which there is only one: Nissen) must recall it; the uninitiated (the rest of us) must invent it. The game has no end.

III

What Nissen makes are altars, idols, temples, ruins, machines, ships, fountains... each, the moment it is recognized, turning into another.

The two basic shapes on which he rings his countless variations are the truncated pyramid and the pillar. The truncated pyramid comes, of course, from the Maya, and Nissen plays, as they did, with the harmonies and contrasts of the simple base and what was placed on the flat top (altars, idols, columns, friezes, falsefronts). It has often been remarked that theMayan pyramids are less works of architecture than sculpture built on a monumental scale. One can imagine them a foot high— the height of a Nissen sculpture— as one could imagine certain of Nissen's pieces as hundreds of feet high, as architecture. And more: the slender pyramids of Tikal (for example), topped with their high combs, mimic a Maya head with its flattened forehead and elaborate headdress. So Nissen's "Pod," a stack of pea pods placed on a blank base, is simultaneously a fantastic Mayan pyramid, an altar on which the pods have been placed, and the blank face and extravagant headdress of an imaginary Pea Goddess— a goddess

72

of fertility and harvest whose last incarnation may well be Carmen Miranda.

The vegetation, the plant forms, that rise out of so many of Nissen's sculptures— as well as the crumbled walls, the gaps (like aboriginal "x-ray" painting) revealing the tombs of images within— cannot help but recall the particularly English preoccupation with ruins. It is an obsession whose earliest record is the Anglo-Saxon poem "The Ruin," a rumination on the rubble of the Roman city of Aquae Sulis (now Bath). An obsession that reached its heights with the Romantics, after the translation in 1795 of Volney's *The Ruins, or a Meditation on the Cycles of Empires*— one of the four books given to educate Frankenstein's monster, and a book that leads directly to Shelley's "Ozymandias" or Wordsworth's "Tintern Abbey." One thinks of the architect Sir John Soane, contemporary to these poets, submitting three sketches of his design for the Bank of England: in the first, the Bank appears brand-new and gleaming; in the second, it is ivy-covered, with weathered stones; in the third, the time is a thousand years later, and the Bank is a stately ruin.

The Romantics saw ruins as emblems of the transitoriness of power, the permanence of nature, the destructive force of greed and corruption, the chaos of the heart overwhelming the orderliness of the intellect. It is possible to ascribe such allegorical meanings to Nissen's sculptures, but they are unlikely. In the first place, the work begins as a transformation of what he literally saw in Mexico: buildings half in rubble, overwhelmed by roots and branches. What matters is not the allegorical (that is, literary) interpretation but rather the fact of metamorphosis itself: the temple that becomes a plant that becomes a bronze.

That play of stone, vegetable and metal brings another element into these sculptures: machines. There are works here called

"Metronome," "Hydrant," even "Jacuzzi." Some of the pieces are simultaneously reminiscent of both the severely truncated versions of the pyramids (the raised platforms in the Great Plaza of Copan, for example) and, an identical shape, the office typewriters of the 1920's.

One thinks of the great debates in the Machine Age of the 1920's and 1930's between the advocates of the machine as the ultimate icon of the new age— a progressive art to celebrate human progress— and those who argued for the perennial centrality of the organic (then called the "biomorphic"). Hart Crane, carrying the argument to literature, attempted to reconcile the two: "For unless poetry can absorb the machine, i.e. *acclimatize* it as naturally and casually as trees, cattle, galleons, castles and all other human associations of the past, then poetry has failed of its full contemporary function." It is interesting to see how, fifty years later, that acclimatization is complete in work like Nissen's— it is not even a question. His "Typewriter" is composed of submarine vegetation; his "Fern" grows razors; his "Zempoala" is a pyramid (in the Totonac site of that name) excavated by Nissen and a tool box; his "Jacuzzi" is adorned with the rings that are washers that are the hoops protruding from the blank walls of the Maya ball courts that are the life preservers on a ship.

Anyone familiar with Mexican art will hear the numerous echoes and rhymes in Nissen's sculpture: the anthropomorphic columns of Tula, the diamond patterning of the Nunnery in Uxmal and the saw-toothed combs of its House of Pigeons, the hooked nose of the rain god Chac protruding from the temples of Chichen Itza and Kabah. They are not— as in the case of the great Mexican muralists— meant to be folkloric, or glorifications of a national past. (It is, of course, neither Nissen's nation nor his past.) Nor are they meant— as the Surrealists used African and Oceanic imagery— as icons of another reality to transport us to dream and the archaic. They are never literal.

What Nissen makes are fetishes: objects of power, objects that look at us looking at them. The source of a fetish's power is accumulation: traditionally each supplicant added something to it, and its strength was the sum of all the individual histories attached to it. Nissen, although he remains the sole "author," reproduces that accumulation in each work.Working with a vocabulary of elemental signs, he heaps layers of history that crumble one into another and become entangled with weeds.

They are idols whose attributes are not quite remembered; maquettes for the monuments of a future civilization; machines with obscure functions; altars for a household shrine. They are objects to be buried with.

....

NOTES FOR *SULFUR* II

[*Written for the back pages of* Sulfur, 1987-1988.]

....

Birkerts vs. Ashbery

[Contributors were asked to respond to a negative article on John Ashbery in the same issue by the critic Sven Birkerts.]

What I find remarkable about Birkerts' piece is its willful ignorance of much of the century, including, most obviously, French poetry. He writes as though Apollinaire and Reverdy, Larbaud and Roussel, Breton, Jacob, Soupault and Char had never existed, or that Ashbery had never read them. His dichotomy of Surrealism ("the transcription of spontaneously recovered, a-logical unconscious materials") and Ashbery ("a calibrated verbal contraption") is false. Despite various claims for the former, the Surrealists were clearly, like all poets, constructing the latter. And Birkerts' isolated praise of Ashbery (the poems "weave a spell, enlarge our sense of mystery... We feel a blurring of bounds, a subjective liberation from the constraints of order") has been equally applied to the Surrealists. Surely one of the important developments of poetry in this century (and particularly in America since the Second World War) is a true internationalism, unseen since the European late Middle Ages. At its worst, it has produced imitators: the American bad Eastern European poet, the South American bad beatnik poet, the Chinese bad imagist. At its best we are seeing legitimate heirs who are transforming the tradition, while working in another language. To my mind, two of the most interesting French poets today happen to write in English: Ashbery and Michael Palmer. That this may strike some as an insult is a result of the continuing mesmerizing effect of Williams' nationalistic jingoism: "American speech." [Everyday American was a language only occasionally employed by Williams, only parodically by Pound and Zukofsky, and almost never by H.D., Moore, Stevens, Crane, Oppen, Olson, et al. Interestingly, its main practitioners— Fearing, Rakosi, Hughes, Blackburn, Reznikoff, Baraka— are considered "minor" poets.]

Furthermore, Birkerts seems strangely oblivious to some recent developments. He should spend an afternoon in the deep shade of *In the American Tree*: Ashbery will seem a fountain of light. After all, an Ashbery poem has an unmistakable (however "impersonal") *voice*— a major verboten in language-land— and an unmistakable atmosphere of oneiric melancholia. I have trouble following Birkerts' exasperation: the passages he quotes seem perfectly comprehensible to me. But perhaps, like many critics, Birkerts is too smart. (Or perhaps, like many readers, I've become stupefied from watching too many flocks of untethered signifiers).

What Birkerts doesn't discuss is the apparent impetus for his piece: Ashbery's extraordinary reputation. That Ashbery has become the most heavily laureled American poet since Lowell, rather than remaining an idiosyncratic worker with a cult following (like, say, Jack Spicer) is unfathomable. It is one of the little mysteries of contemporary American poetry. Calling out the deconstructionists, as Birkerts does, doesn't help: they have made each other's reputations, not those of any writer, and Ashbery would have existed without them. I have no answer; I doubt Ashbery himself could explain; it's one of those things.

Finally, I find Birkerts' version of the growth of language, both in the individual and in the species, unconvincing. There is no "condition of confused unknowing" before language, for there is no species without a language and there is only one confused species. Language did not "evolve to remove us from" confusion: it put us there. (One of its mutations, poetry, sometimes gets us out.) As for the individual, it seems to me that language is acquired more in delight and play than out of frustration, and further, that the world is only as complex as one's language. One must have a sophisticated language to invent meaninglessness, and I'm surprised that the baby Birkerts yearned for meaning, and felt that "the world overran" his grasp of it. I'll take his word on it, but I suspect that such highchair existentialism is quite rare.

[1987]

....

A *Brief Note on* Montemora, *America & the World*

In Jed Rasula's excellent essay on Robert Bly in *Sulfur* 19— forever memorable for the phrase

"Age of Acquarius"— I was surprised to see mention of *Montemora*, a magazine I edited from 1975 to 1982. But I'm afraid I find his characterization somewhat misleading.

First, I shudder to think that *Montemora* was the "only comparable effort" in the 1970's to Bly's *The Sixties*. I have never had much interest in any of Bly's countless productions. [He is probably our Longfellow— a sentimentalist poet, an enthusiast for Northern Europe and the American wilderness, a bad translator from many languages— though I doubt he ever wrote a line as memorable as "By the shores of Gitchy-Goomee."] For me, the "models" among the regularly published magazines of the 1960's were *Caterpillar*, above all; *Kulchur,* whose critical essays were far nastier, wittier and on-target than anything in *The Sixties*; and that great Representative Work, *Poetry* under the editorship of Henry Rago, which was everything a magazine like *American Poetry Review* should be. (Not to mention the scores of lively short-lived magazines; a flowering that hasn't been seen since.)

Second, it is simply untrue that *Montemora* had "a minimal involvement with domestic poetry." Though such nationalistic distinctions make me queasy, I would guess that two-thirds of the magazine was devoted to writing by or about my fellow Americans.

Montemora was basically a repertory company with occasional guest appearances. The cast included George and Mary Oppen, Reznikoff, Rakosi, Bronk, Sobin, Duncan, DuPlessis, Rothenberg, Eshleman, Lessing, Tarn, Corman, Kleinzahler, S. Howe, Baraka, Enslin, Kirschen, Greene, R. Waldrop, among others. Some of these, surprisingly, were not being published elsewhere at the time; others were appearing in print for the first time. There were also extensive selections of unpublished material by the dead masters (Loy, Niedecker, Zukofsky, Pound, H.D.).

Poets who, for whatever reason, were not contributors, were discussed in critical articles (Antin, Eigner, R. Johnson, Palmer, Rexroth, MacLow, Dorn, et al). And the magazine published seven books that were sent free to subscribers, all of them by gringos and five of them first books (DuPlessis, Lessing, two by Sobin, Mary Oppen, Kirschen, Susan Howe). As a map of American poetry, I now regret certain omissions, but not the general topography.

Of course there was a great deal of, um, *foreign* poetry. The repertory company included a half-dozen interesting young British poets who haven't appeared on these shores since; Chinese and Japanese translations by Burton Watson, Hiroaki Sato, A.C. Graham and Jonathan Chaves; classical French translations by Jonathan Griffin and Paul Auster; Jabès, Bunting, MacDiarmid, Roy Fisher, Paz, Césaire, Turnbull, Montale, Huidobro, Jaccottet, Blanchot, and on & on. The idea was a single perspective drawing from a variety of sources, regardless of original language. Curiously, *Montemora* is remembered— if at all— as a translation magazine.

Since 1960 there have been only three such international magazines: *Caterpillar, Alcheringa*, and *Montemora*. They died in 1973, 1977, and 1982, respectively. That nothing has replaced them is the result of a disturbing development: translation is no longer an activity practiced by poets, particularly those of the (more or less) "avant-garde."

The two golden ages of English-language poetry (roughly 1550 to 1650 and 1910 to when? 1970?) were not coincidentally eras of intense translating. Consider, in the latter period, the amazing range of poets who published at least one book-length translation: Pound, Williams, H.D., Yeats, Eliot, Moore, Auden, Spender, Stein, Rexroth, Aldington, L. Hughes, MacDiarmid,

Zukofsky, A. Lowell, R. Lowell, Schwartz, Jarrell, E. Bishop, MacNeice, Day Lewis, Campbell, Rukeyser, Gregory, Bynner, Spicer, Merton, Blackburn, Dorn, Eshleman, Tarn, Rothenberg, Snyder, Ashbery, Corman, Tomlinson, Levertov, Hollo, Logue, Middleton, Merwin, Bly, Strand, Griffin, J. Wright, Harwood, Padgett, Roditi, Simic, Gascoyne, Barnard, Schwerner, Economou, Reynolds, Turnbull, Wilbur, T. Hughes...

And those who translated occasionally: Reznikoff, Stevens, Bunting, Tate, Empson, Cummings, Crane, Cunard, J.P. Bishop, Housman, Raine, Masefield, Millay, Hardy, Watkins, Ginsberg, Duncan, Antin, Kelly, Kunitz, Hollander, Hall, Ferlinghetti, Ignatow, Oppen, Cunningham, Sorrentino, Laughlin... Or embedded translations in their work: Olson, David Jones...

And the novelists or prose writers who translated poetry: Nabokov, Dos Passos, Fitzgerald, Ford, Boyle, Joyce, Beckett, Kipling, Santayana, Josephson, Cowley, Chesterton, K.A. Porter, Davenport, Waldo Frank, P. Bowles...

In fact, the difficult list to make is those who never translated poetry: Loy, Niedecker, O'Hara (?), D. Thomas, Bronk, Baraka, Creeley, McClure...

Then take a look at the Ron Silliman anthology, *In the American Tree*, which serves as a handy roster of the contemporary avant-garde, both for the 44 poets included and— a far more interesting group— the 80 excluded poets of "comparable worth" listed in the preface. Of those 124— excluding Lydia Davis, a prose writer who translates prose— only one, Rosmarie Waldrop, translates on a regular basis. Only a few others have done some occasional translations. What has happened?

It's my belief that, in the 1980's, Reaganism has infected every particle of life in this country, not excluding the life and work of poets, no matter how much they may hold him in contempt. As such, the Silliman anthology is an expression of Reagan America much as Donald Allen's *The New American Poetry* (1960) was, in many ways, an expression of Eisenhower America. In an era of rampant nationalism and xenophobia (whose examples I need hardly enumerate) we have an anthology of new writing so nationalistic and so xenophobic that it salutes America in its title, divides its poets more or less along state lines, and deliberately excludes some excellent poets who had the misfortune to be born a few miles north of the border. Nor is the Silliman anthology an isolated aberration: it is rare in the extensive critical writings of the "language" poets to encounter any reference to foreign poetry outside of Russian Futurism.

Further, the stylistic gesture most characteristic of "language" writing is the non-sequitur (which is quite different, it should be said, from Cubist simultaneity, Surrealist collage, or the Poundian ideogrammic method). It is the product of a generation raised in front of a television: an endless succession of depthless images and empty sounds, each canceling the previous one. A non-sequitur implies a loss of memory, an erasing of history. "Language" poetry as it is practiced by its strictest followers is identical to the speech of television's masterpiece, Ronald Reagan: words set free of any possible meanings, sentences that ignore or contradict what has just been said, words whose effect is not meant to go beyond the second in which they are uttered: words without history.

In Reagan America there has been only one important study of pre-20th century poetry written by a poet: Susan Howe's *My Emily Dickinson*. (How many articles has *Sulfur* published on poetry before 1900?) There has been only one major new translation of a classic (Western) text: Richard Sieburth's Hölderlin. There are only two "avant-garde" poets who continue to trans-

.

late regularly: Waldrop and Eshleman. Such a state would have been inconceivable to Pound, Williams, H.D., Rexroth, Eliot, Zukofsky, Olson... poets inseparable from their own versions of history and the places they found for themselves on the world map.

[1987]

....

The "Language" Letters

[*The preceding note provoked an open letter from Michael Davidson in defense of "language" poetry. His letter and my response (part one, below) and his response to it were circulated to a few* Sulfur *contributors. Comments by Rachel Blau DuPlessis and Clayton Eshleman, as well as a speech to the* MLA *by Ron Silliman, were published; a long* ad hominem *by Charles Bernstein was withdrawn by its author (and later recycled into a poem that eliminated my name and the context, but retained the pejorative phrases). These were followed by my reply (part two, below). For the other texts, see* Sulfur #22, Spring 1988.]

I

Dear Michael,

As your letter was intended for publication in *Sulfur*, I'll similarly switch into public debate mode...

1. First, a matter of definition. "Language" poetry is a term generally understood by everyone who is not a "language" poet.

(Indeed, the one unmistakable sign of a "language" poet is the denial that "language" poetry exists.) Although it is now breaking up from the inevitable power struggles that occur when individual artists or writers realize the limitations of group identity, it was, in its day, the most organized literary movement, ever, on American soil. Some forty or fifty poets, running twenty or thirty small presses and magazines, produced a mountain of printed matter, almost entirely limited to work by or about members of the group. This in turn led to a number of anthologies— by and of members— in mainstream magazines and larger and university presses, countless appearances at academic symposia, and a stream of favorable critical commentary from professor-critics. Which led to a remarkable amount of publicity, from the vinyl heights of airline "in-flight" magazines to the sewers of right-wing publications like *Partisan Review* and *The New Criterion*.

Yet this enormous hoopla never translated into much of a readership, even within the small world of poetry. The last time an anti-establishment poetry movement was in the news, its major gathering (Donald Allen's *New American Poetry*) sold 100,000 copies. In contrast, the three most accessible introductions to the movement, Bernstein and Andrews' *The LANGUAGE Book* [only fanatics have the patience to type in all those equal-signs], Messerli's *"Language" Poetries*, and Silliman's *In the American Tree* have, I understand, sold around a thousand copies each. (It is not, of course, a measure of aesthetic importance, but rather of a genuine public interest.)

2. Discussions of "language" poetry are, for me, always skewed by the inclusion of Clark Coolidge, Susan Howe and Michael Palmer in the various "language" anthologies and magazines. (And many defenders of "language" tend to summon up Coolidge, Howe and Palmer when the going gets rough.) Their

presence is surely the product of personal and not group affinities. Each of the three, in utterly different ways, is far beyond (or actively contrary to) the proscriptions of Perelman, Andrews, Watten, Silliman, et al. Coolidge is obviously a direct descendent of Louis Zukofsky— without sharing Zukofsky's love of hidden organizing principles and multilayered reference. His intense musicality, a combination of Elizabethan lyricism and the improvisations of bebop, is unlike anything else in "language"-land. Howe, through her poetry and critical writings, has become the great (and probably the last) poet of a certain thread of American history and myth— the true heir to Olson. Palmer comes directly out of Cubism and Surrealism, with lessons learned from Spicer, Creeley, the "objectivists," Celan, Jabès, and many others. Taken together, the three represent a continuation of modernist preoccupations with musical structure, dreams, history, myth, psychology, image, dialogues with the dead, and the invention of a "personal" style dependent on a hyper-referential ("charged") language— all stuff the "language" poets are generally attempting to shred.

So I exclude all three in talking in general about "language" poetry, as well as Jackson MacLow (whose inclusion in the Messerli anthology is rather like the Red Brigades bestowing honorary membership on Jean-Paul Sartre); the street-smart, funny, erotic, utterly unobscure Bernadette Mayer (whose presence in the Silliman book I can't understand), and the two writers of crystalline narrative prose, Robert Gluck and Lydia Davis, whose appearance in the "language" poetry canon is the greatest mystery of all. Once these, quite different, writers are separated out, what's left is an extraordinarily cohesive set of practices and concerns, one that coheres beyond the enthusiasms of individual members for writers outside the group.

3. Once, just once, someone should write a defense of "language" poetry without employing the words *trope, paratactic, temporality, historiography, semantic, semiologic, reification, dehistoricization, teleological, dialectical, syllogism, figuration, rhetoric of equivalence, homology, strategy.* (All of these in your 2 1/2 page letter!)

Given that "language" poetry represents itself as a radical critique of the dominant political / linguistic / philosophical / narrative / spiritual / economic power structures, I have never understood why it insistently explains itself in such jargon-enstrangled prose. In a recent article on Steve McCaffery (*Temblor* #6), Marjorie Perloff, a "language" supporter, claims that the "ugliness, the intentional ungainliness" of the prose written by McCaffery, Bernstein, Andrews, Dreyer, and Armantrout— she adds Silliman later, but forgets Watten— should be seen as a reaction against both the "genteel" art of the literary essay, as practiced by an Edmund Wilson or a Randall Jarrell(literature for the middlebrow non-specialist) and the "casual, speech-based, notebook or diary-style poetics of the Beats and New York poets." True perhaps, but these are hardly the only options: the century is full of models of radical critical prose: in English by Stein, Pound, Loy, Lawrence, Olson, and Susan Howe; in French by Tzara, Artaud, Bataille, and Leiris; or in Spanish by Huidobro, Lezama Lima, and Paz (to name a few of the obvious).

Curiously, Perloff identifies the "genteel" style as "Oxbridge" and "Ivy League." "Oxbridge" it may remain, but in fact, the technocratic prose of the "language" poets is precisely the kind of writing practiced by the English Departments of the Ivy League, particularly Yale. The rise of "language" poetry occurs exactly at the moment when the English Department was split in two: one branch remaining as the Eng. Dept., and the other as the Creative Writing Program. What its detractors still label as "academic" poetry— the stuff published in *APR*, *Antaeus*, etc.— is the product of Creative Writing. I would argue that there are now two other "academic" poetries, which reflect, in turn, the warring old and new factions in the remaining Eng. Dept.: the new traditional prosodists (Leithauser, Gioia, et al) championed by *The New Criterion*, and the "language" poets, who are, many of them, the only literary practitioners of deconstruction. (Though ultimately there may be more similarities than differences between the two: aren't both the New Augustans?)

Of course few of them actually work full-time in the university— though they are the first avant-gardists to be "conference" regulars. But by their wholesale acceptance of its critical tenets, as well as its prose style,specialized language, self-referentiality and disdain for the uninitiated, the "language" poets have formed their own autonomous English Department of the Spirit— and one, as might be expected, full of intradepartmental politics.

To my mind it is precisely this sectarianism— quite similar to certain ultra- factions of the New Left in the late 60's— that has led to the general ill-will felt toward "language" poets. When one picks up a "language" anthology or magazine, one knows exactly who will be included, who will be writing about whom, and in what manner. It is more predictable than *Antaeus*. There has been little attempt to widen the literary context in which the "language" poets locate themselves, or to explain themselves in what the hopelessly *démodé* rest of the world considers as accessible prose. It is a kind of self-containment that would have been unimaginable to the most elitist of the modernists, who, after all, spent a great deal of time preaching to the unconverted.

4. Strangely enough, perhaps the only objective comment in my piece has drawn the loudest protests from readers. To repeat,

of the forty-odd poets included in Silliman's *Tree* and the eighty "others"— largely unaffiliated avant-gardists— that he lists, only Rosmarie Waldrop (an "other") publishes substantial poetry translations on a regular basis. This is of course absolutely true. A few of the others have done a few occasional translations, some of them excellent, but none of them are a significant means of access to a foreign poet or body of work. This situation is, as I wrote, general to the avant-garde, "langs" and non-"langs" alike, and has, I think, already proven detrimental.

Translation aside, naturally I recognize that, as you say, "foreign writing has made its impact" on "language" poetry, if by "writing" one means "critical theory"— a crucial difference. But it is obvious that foreign poetry— with the occasional exception of Russian Futurism— has not. If one calculated the total number of pages in LANGUAGE, *Tottel's*, *Roof*, *This*, etc. devoted in any way to foreign-language poetry, I doubt it would barely reach into two figures. To me, this is a self-absorption bordering on nationalism and xenophobia. How else do you explain the exclusion of even (gasp!) Canadian writers as essential to the movement as McCaffery and Dewdney from Silliman's *Tree* and the Messerli book? How else do you explain why Silliman's *Tree* is American at all? Movement anthologies— Imagism, Others, Objectivism, etc— are traditionally transnational (even Rimbaud was an "objectivist"!). By limiting themselves to Americans— and Silliman even divides his book into "East" and "West"— the two anthologists are implying that all that's happening in this New Aesthetic is happening in this land.)

Furthermore, I have always been amazed that a movement so preoccupied with language shows no interest whatsoever in specific languages. It would, to take an obvious example, be extremely interesting to see a "language" response to Chinese poetry, which is dependent both on a multiplicity of meaning in the individual ideogram, and the placement of what were known as "empty" (meaningless) words. (And the groundwork is already there in François Cheng's *Chinese Poetic Writing*.) Or, say, something on Sanskrit (where, according to Ingalls, the sentence "Although she was embarrassed by the earnest glance of the king, still out of curiosity it was slowly that she walked away from him, looking backward as she walked" may be expressed in three words; where it is not uncommon for a word to have two or three hundred exact synonyms; where, without resorting to synonyms, a sentence like "Go get my horse" may be written fifteen different ways). Or, assuming they've all read Whorf, something on Native American or other indigenous languages. "Language" may have a few more women than previous movements, but it is still unrepentantly honkey in both its makeup and outlook.

5. In a similar vein, to claim that the "language" poets' "literary interests are broader than the English/American tradition" is stretching it. With the notable exception of Susan Howe (whom I don't think is a "language" poet anyway), I see little evidence in their writings of much interest in even the English/American tradition before the 20th century at all. (For example: 8 of the 464 pages of Bernstein's *Content's Dream* are on Blake and Shakespeare; in the 236 pages of Watten's *Total Syntax* there is a passing reference each to Coleridge and Dickinson.) The rediscovery or reevaluation of earlier poets was once essential to a personal poetics, whether one was Zukofsky or Eliot, Robert Duncan or Allen Tate. This has simply not occurred with any of the "language" poets. (It's incredible that, after fifteen years, no one has mentioned "language"'s greatest precursor: John Skelton.)

6. What I mean by the "non-sequitur" is Cubist simultaneity, Surrealist collage and the Poundian ideogrammic method in its

decadent stage. Your "alternate forms of temporality," "critiques of narrative logic," etc.were news around 1912 ("Zone"). Since then, "techniques of radical juxtaposition" may be the one distinguishing characteristic of nearly all "avant-garde" poetry written in this century. Those fragments of a whole were, however, a Utopic yearning for a whole. Now the "language" poets have exploded the myth of the whole, and what seems to be left is what television calls "bites": very short bits of glitzy images or catchy phrases that are dependent on immediate effect. A "language" poem in perhaps its most typical form begins, ends, and goes nowhere (utopia?) and consists of short wisecracks, epigrams, bits of slang or advertising slogans or popular songs, gnomic remarks, ironic references to suburban American culture, etc., all held together by a glue of impenetrable declarative sentences or seemingly random word-lists. Some of the "bites" are arresting— and they usually turn up in the reviews of "language" poets. Many of the "bites" are funny. (Strange that their wit appears only in the poetry, never in the critical prose.) But in the end it seems to me no different from rock video, which the industry calls "moving wallpaper." Were it not for the ponderousness of its defensive prose, much of "language" poetry could easily be seen as a kind of moving-wallpaper literature for the current generation of grad students who were raised in front of the tube— a harmless entertainment not unlike the "7 types of ambiguity" poetry produced for students in the 1950's.

7. The "real agenda" of my article was not, as you imagine, world domination of literary production by the Lionel Trilling Cultural Brigade. Unlike critics and "language" poets, I have no agenda at all: I read books. But I do believe that the concentration on "language" poetry, both for and against, has tended to drown out everything else on the aesthetic left. For the first time

in twenty years, for example, I am aware of excellent poets who cannot get published in book form anywhere, large or small press— let alone discussed, even in the little magazines.

Also missing is any sense of the young. Where is the anthology for them? Most of the poets in the "language" anthologies are in their forties or older. (The poets of *The New American Poetry* were largely in their twenties or thirties.) There seems to be an "aging" of poetry matching the demographic aging of America. Take the little magazine, traditionally a young person's work. (Who else has the passion, the time, and the dedication for such drudgery?) At the moment, the best poetry magazines are edited by people in their forties and fifties: *Sulfur, Temblor, Hambone, (How)ever.* I know two interesting magazines with editors in their thirties, *Acts* and *House of K*, but I am unaware of any substantial magazine run by anyone in her or his twenties.

To my mind, a revitalization of the American poetry "avant-garde" will only occur when the young appear with fresh readings of their living elders, rediscovering the neglected— think of all the discoveries of the 1960's: Niedecker, Oppen, Zukofsky, Loy, Reznikoff, Bunting, Rakosi, H.D.—and presenting themselves in the context of those they admire. A new generation of restless disciples that will pick up the threads of the "New American" poets, the *Caterpillar* generation, and the isolated individuals who have emerged since. One that will discover all that's been happening in world poetry since American poets generally stopped translating. (And the place to start is Latin America.) One that will discover its own models in the English/American tradition. And, most important, one that finds the world interesting, that sees the world as something more than a problematic text. Now that we've said that it can't be said, there are many other things to say.

91

II

Literary movements have traditionally had three functions: First, the criticism of the prevailing aesthetic, which is usually the aesthetic of the preceding generation. Second, the proposal of a new aesthetic and the promotion of its practitioners. Third, the introduction of other, historical or foreign, work: discoveries of neglected masters in the same language, new readings or translations of well-known texts, translations of the previously untranslated. This third function is both a service to the community and a means of historical or international validation for the new aesthetic: a new context in which to locate the new. Thus, a tiny movement like Imagism simultaneously soured the appreciation of late 19th century texts, promoted a handful of new poets, and forever changed the way classical Greek and Chinese poems were read and translated. Thus, one of the projects of a huge movement like Surrealism— which revolutionized taste on all aesthetic fronts— was the introduction of a wide range of non-Western texts: Latin American writers, to take a small example, had to go to Paris in the 1920's to "discover" pre-Columbian oral and written literature. Thus, the one truly enduring aspect of the New Criticism may well be its bringing of the Metaphysical poets back onto the map.

The members of the "language" movement have been hyperactive in fulfilling the first two functions. They have attempted to dismantle the prevailing aesthetic— what Ron Silliman, in his MLA (of course!) paper modestly calls "the naive assumption of speech, individualism or 'beauty.'" They have tirelessly promoted a new aesthetic and its practitioners. What they haven't done is bring any other (non-critical) writings into the fold. This is not to suggest that they are individually ill-read— far from it. But in their voluminous writings and public speeches, they have generally ignored everyone except themselves, a few non-affiliated contemporaries, and the French and German critics currently fashionable among art critics and English professors. "Language," for me at least, would be an exciting and genuinely challenging movement if it presented its own idiosyncratic historical "canon," revisionary readings of the classics, discoveries of lost masters, bridges to previously unknown foreign poets, commentaries not only on language but on languages. This has simply not occurred as a collective effort.

To my mind there have been four movements (or tendencies or constellations) in America since 1960 which have not only produced important poetry, but have been extraordinarily enriching for those not active in the group:

—The black nationalist poetry of the 1960's, which, besides its political agenda, effectively admitted black speech into poetry (something the Harlem Renaissance poets, with the notable exception of Hughes, had refused to do), created a large and genuinely populist audience for poetry, had a close and exciting working relationship with jazz and some rock musicians (still extent, in pop form, as rap and hip-hop), offered scathing commentaries on white "verse," and brought in a great deal of African and Afro-American history, mythology and religion which had previously been absent in American poetry.

—The poetry written and read against the Vietnam War, that unique moment when American poets served as citizens, witnesses, intellectual consciences of the nation (a role that poets routinely perform elsewhere on the planet). Most important, a moment when political necessity compelled a settling of differences among the poetry communities: not only between academic and non-academic, but among the non-academics. (It has been forgotten, especially by Silliman, that the Donald Allen anthology was intended as a peaceable kingdom for the bitterly warring factions of the anti-establishment: though it is difficult for us to sort out now, the Black Mountains hated the Beats and so on.) The readings and anthologies against the War were a truly democratic vision of a republic of letters, and, as Clayton Eshleman says here, seemed to portend a "responsible avant-garde" for the post-Vietnam years.

—Ethnopoetics— essentially an American revision and expansion of Surrealism— which not only introduced a tremendous amount of indigenous material, but also presented a re-reading of American literature, discovered all sorts of strange and forgotten poets, emphasized oral performance and poetry rituals and talismans, translated a great deal of European modernist poets, offered new theories and practices of translation, and, perhaps most of all, proposed an image of the poet, based on the archaic, as a vital, necessary member of the community.

—Finally, the women poets who are currently centered around the magazine *HOW(ever)*. After the isolated work of Dickinson, H.D., Loy, Stein and Niedecker, it is a concentrated and collective effort to challenge the inherited (patriarchal) language, invent a feminine and feminist language of poetry and new modes of criticism, reread and reconsider the entire history of poetry, and raise the pioneer women modernists to their rightful positions of importance. To my mind this is the most exciting group activity occurring in American poetry today. (Though one that desperately needs more periodical outlets.)

What these four movements have given me is a tremendous sense of worlds opening up. (And I should emphasize that I am

94

speaking of group activity as a sum of all the individual efforts involved— obviously no single individual can do everything.) That black nationalism and ethnopoetics have produced no viable second generations, and that the Vietnam War poetry led nowhere, is, for me, the great disaster of American poetry in the late 1970's and 1980's.

[Given the current obsession with criticism— Silliman's italicized *"writing itself is not sufficient for completeness in poetry"* being the latest pronouncement— it should be said that all of these movements have promoted "critical thinking," though their rhetoric bears no resemblance to "language" discourse. And Silliman is way off when he states that the "New Americans" were against critical thinking: true perhaps of Corso or Ferlinghetti, but Duncan, Olson, Creeley, Levertov, Dorn, Jones/Baraka, Snyder, Sorrentino? All published at least one book of critical essays, and many of the others wrote isolated articles.]

On the other hand, what "language" as a movement has given me is the sense of worlds being closed off. That reductionist label "language" or "language-centered" says it all. One can only imagine how they will react to Rachel DuPlessis, in her statement here, raising words like *pleasure, transcendence, passion, feeling.*

For me, a model of the life and work of a poet was Robert Duncan, who died yesterday— a poet who embraces all the words on DuPlessis' list and much more: curiosity, pluralism, history, indignation, spirituality, social and moral accountability. I have never gotten over the first (now famous) words of Duncan's that I ever read, in the first *Caterpillar*, 21 years ago: "The drama of our time is the coming of all men into one fate..." and his dream of a "symposium of the whole" where all "the old excluded orders must be included: the female, the proletariat, the foreign; the animal and vegetative; the unconscious and unknown;

the criminal and failure." That Duncan, toward the end, found no room at his symposium for the "language" poets was, I think, a mistake— even though nearly all of them stand in opposition to nearly all of his beliefs. A symposium of general agreement is no symposium at all.

[1988]

....

IS GOD DOWN?

[Written in 1987— approximately Anno 5 of the personal computer— for an issue of Agni devoted to "Spirituality After Silicon Valley." The editor, Askold Melnyczuk, asked contributors to respond to a statement that read, in part: "What are the promises implicit and explicit in the Gospel of Apple? With all the space… devoted even in the literary press to questions rising around the increasing hegemony of computers and word processors, are we to assume technology has been humanized? Or has humanity been technologized? When we reflect on machines, what is it we are reflecting on? Is the ghost in the machine a plausible structure for a shapelier muse? Or does it aim merely to keep us amused? More specifically, how in 1987 is the spiritual life affected by the (divinization of the) computer?"]

Leaving aside the separate issue of the relation between the computer and literature, Askold Melnyczuk's paragraph seems to break into four, somewhat contradictory, questions: In the age of computers, is the machine divine? is the machine more human? is the human less human? is the divine less divine?

The computer may be an international obsession, but it is hardly a religious phenomenon, as Melnyczuk suggests. Religion generally implies a supernatural (non-empirical) explanation and a celebration of the order of the universe and the mysteries of life and death.

The computer, however extraordinary as a tool for computation, compilation and measurement,offers no such explanations. Nor is it a sacred being in the non-Western sense, an incarnation of a super-natural force. We may marvel at its superior calculating capabilities, but this is human programming, not the wisdom of the gods. We may tremble and rage before it— particularly when a "glitch" dyna-mites a bank account or a monthly bill— but it is then no wrathful Old Testament god, but merely the non-human agent of inhuman bureaucracy (or, at its most malign, of state surveillance).

It has of course been a force in psychological change. To spend one's day working with a computer is a narcissistic, masturbatory pleasure. Although it is a stickler for details, the computer, unlike messy humans, always answers immediately, and always answers yes or no. The yes is instantly gratifying, and the no, after refram-ing the question or rethinking one's own logic, can usually be transformed into a yes. Unlike the video arcade where one always loses, where the object is to delay defeat, at the computer one nearly always ultimately wins. This is all quite different from dealing with humans, those stubborn and vague creatures, and the transition from facing a monitor to facing a face can be diffi-cult. The 1980's, as it has been said so many times, is the decade of "me," of greed, of the Trivial Pursuit of happiness and the anx-iety of "coping," and now of a generally unwarranted fear (that is, among those who are most hysterical: the heterosexual middle class majority) of the other as carrier of a lethal disease. An age of a self-absorbed, distracted solitude, where the real is either hostile or remote. This probably would not have occurred without the computer in the workplace and the television at home.

It may be a desocialization, but is it a dehumanization? I was surprised that Melnyczuk raised yet again that perennial sympo-sium topic (now approaching its bicentennial): are humans becoming more like machines? are we less human? Our wars may now be masked by technological euphemisms ("Pentagonese") but it is still war business as usual, and as cruel as ever. The workers who construct microchips or Oldsmobiles are no more or less like machines than the workers who constructed the pyramids. The secretary stares with the same blankness at a monitor, a typewriter, or a sheaf of paper written with a quill pen. Most work is deadening: it was a mistake of Romanticism to find the machine more deadening. (Wordsworth, unlike his neighbors, never spent a 16-hour day pitching hay.) The real question is not the dehumanizing effect of technology, but rather the dehumanizing effect of work. Revolutions have succeeded in improving the material well-being of workers, but they have never changed the nature of work, have never made it spiritually satisfying. (The closest they've come, in this century, is nationalism as a kind of state religion, a spirit of enthusiasm for mundane tasks that rarely outlasts the first generation— those who remember how bad things were before.) We have to go back to Fourier to find a system of collective labor based intrinsically on human nature.

The human is no less human, but the divine— the Western divine— may at the moment be less divine, and not in the obvious way. The computer has so accelerated the Enlightenment that we have barely realized where we have landed. The extraordinary speed and precision of its measurements and calculations have not only failed to fully and "rationally" explain the universe(thus killing off God), they have uncovered more mysteries than ever were imagined. There has never been a society more capable of describing the physical world, and yet there has never been a society more bewildered by it. The order of the universe turns out to be more divine than our (Western) image of it. Small wonder the physicists are sounding like theologians these days.

Human nature can only take so much inexplicability, and it seems inevitable that a new world religion will arise in the coming centuries (if we make it that far). Certainly Islam, Judaism and Christianity— those magnificent dream-structures of shepherds and desert villagers— are inadequate to the task. All three, in their institutionalized form, are dependent on dogmatic rigidity, the suppression of heterodoxy, separation and exclusion, and a morality progressively basing itself on less wisdom. There is nothing sadder than their current desperate and final waves of fundamentalism: in the Vatican, in Iran, in Israel, in the White House. The Eastern religions, on the other hand, have tended to embrace everything, to adapt almost any development into their cosmic view: the Vedic god Agni is equally incarnate in fire and in a literary magazine. Stripped of their local trappings, they remain remarkably compatible with the latest scientific news, as a number of pop science-religion books have suggested. Nuclear physicists at the Bombay reactor light incense before a statue of Ganesh, the elephant-headed god; a Western scientist who considers herself a Christian has to do a great deal of defensive shuffling, picking and choosing.

1492 dealt the first serious blow to the three monotheisms: the first extended contact with a great mass of people untouched by God. The monotheisms survived by largely destroying the evidence, but in many ways they never fully recovered: the modern era of doubt and criticism was born. The computer— not in itself, but as tool of discovery, an ultra-sophisticated caravel taking us into unimagined and inexplicable information— may well bring an end to the monotheisms, or, at best, force them onto the paths laid out over the centuries by their mystics and heterodox sects. As the millennium approaches, and as the world's population increases with its concomitant suffering, there will be a proliferation of messianic and millenary cults. (It is already the case in Africa.) It is not difficult to imagine one of these merging with a more cerebral, "scientific" religion— much in the way that Taoism and Buddhism, and Christianity in the Third World, have both theoretical and practical sides. On the one hand, a religion that celebrates and explains the mysteries of the new cosmos; on the other, a religion of idols, charms, spells, trances, dancing, music and magic to alleviate the daily worldly suffering.

Finally, the less important question of computers and literature: is the writer a robot, or has the robot become a writer? To take the second question first: certainly the computer has forever proved that a thousand monkeys typing at a thousand typewriters for a thousand years will not produce any *Hamlets*. There are a few serious writers who have made use of the computer (not as "word processor") to "generate" texts, most notably Jackson MacLow and the members of OULIPO. These are not, as might be assumed, impersonal: behind each text is the human who programmed it. The results are weird or amusing, their ultimate pleasure deriving mainly from seeing the rules of the game put into action, like extremely complex poetic forms: *chant royal*, say, or Chinese poems that can be read forwards or backwards.

The typewriter certainly had an effect on the writing of poetry. It is impossible to imagine the stepped lines of Williams, Paz, and so many others without it. Pound's *Cantos* makes much more visible sense in his manuscript than on the printed page, and Robert Duncan has recently insisted that his books directly reproduce his own typed manuscript. With the advent of "desktop publishing," there will no doubt be poems that take advantage of its various features, including the mixing of type styles. Furthermore, the computer has democratized certain tricks of the trade. Auden's far-reaching and witty rhymes lose much of their charm after a glance through the computer-generated *Penguin Rhyming Dictionary* (with its hundred rhymes for "Freud," but only one, "broaden," for "Auden"). Rhyme— lately championed again by young conservatives— becomes more than ever a question of selection rather than invention.

But this is not "word processing," that wonderful phrase that turns writing into packaged cheese. (Poets, said, Chesterton, have been strangely reticent on the subject of cheese.) Word processing is essentially a means of manuscript production that eliminates retyping. A labor-saving device: no more, no less. Yet, like most labor-saving devices, it results in far less labor. In the era of microwave ovens nearly no one has the time to bake their own bread. Before the word processor and the xerox machine, when manuscripts were written out and copied by hand, the triple-decker novel and the book-length poem were the norm— think of Baudelaire's quip that the long poem was the refuge of those incapable of writing short poems— not to mention voluminous diaries and correspondence. Today the standard work is the short story, the minimalist novel, the anecdotal lyric— and who writes long letters? The computer is not, in itself, an obstacle to concentration or inspiration. But this is a time of continual distraction, a result of the huge population and the huge amount of artwork the population is producing. (One creates by forcibly, if only temporarily, refusing to consume.) The entirety of classical Greek literature is now available on a single compact disk. Perhaps the writers of the late 20th century, tapping at their private consoles, should all feed into a giant mainframe that will eliminate the ceaseless repetitions that now fill the magazines, consolidate the texts, and restore us to our rightful role of Anonymous, the voice of the age.

....

PANAMA: A PALINDROME

[*Written as a "Letter from New York" for* Vuelta *magazine
in Mexico, February 1990.*]

"C'est le crach du Panama qui fit de moi un poète!"
Blaise Cendrars, 1914

A man, a plan, a canal: Panama!
It's my favorite palindrome; nearly a hundred years old, and
never out of date, for it seems that Panama is fated to always
have a man— an American man— with a plan. It is a palindrome of our history, a tiny loop forever repeating itself. A
thousand years from now, while the rest of the earth is wearing
white robes and discussing philosophy with Alpha Centauri, the
President of the United States— there will always be a President
and a United States— will no doubt yet again unwrap Teddy
Roosevelt's big stick and clobber that little strip of jungle
cleared for oil tankers and secretive banks.

George Bush declared that the purpose of the invasion was to
"restore democracy" to Panama, and to bring an indicted drug
dealer to trial in Miami. When it was pointed out that the U.S.
normally does not deploy 26,000 troops to arrest a felon, Bush

claimed he was deposing a dictator. When it was pointed out that the U.S. normally does not send 26,000 troops to topple minor despots, Bush replied that he was protecting American children from the scourge of drugs.

Beyond this palindrome of excuses was the usual net of political opportunism and some unusual personal ill-will. Bush claimed that the suddenness of the invasion was due to Noriega's declaration, in some local speech somewhere, of war against the U.S., and the subsequent murder of an American soldier by Panama Defense Force (PDF) troops. It is remarkable that Bush could repeat Noriega's threat with a straight face— but then again, Reagan actually declared a national State of Emergency in response to the awesome malevolency of the Sandinistas, poised to drive their pickups north. As for the dead soldier, the U.S. routinely shrugs off the murder abroad of its citizens, whether they are nuns in El Salvador or 260 Marines in Beirut. (Much later we learned that the invasion had been scheduled weeks in advance, that the soldier was not in uniform and was attempting, for unknown reasons, perhaps inebriation, to drive through a PDF roadblock without stopping.)

The invasion was set in December for one reason: On January 1, according to the terms of the Panama Canal Treaty, the Canal Commission was to have been headed by a Panamanian selected by their own government. (On January 1, 2000, the U.S. will withdraw from the Canal completely.) The treaty has been a leitmotif of Republican outrage—"We built it, it's ours!"—since Jimmy Carter signed it: Reagan used it over and over as a symbol of America's weakness and Carter's wimpiness. For ten years, the right has been trying to figure out how to get the Canal back; with the Commission now remaining under their control, they have another ten to work out some gruesome solution to their day of doom.

It was an act of personal vendetta. Though it is unprecedented for an American President to send thousands of troops to redress a private grievance, Bush, like Reagan and Nixon before him, seems to be modeling himself on the patriarchs of the banana republics: crying out for a return to "law and order" while routinely ignoring the Constitution. (War, after all, is supposed to be approved by Congress before troops are committed, except in cases of immediate threat.) But few Presidents these days seem to have read the manual.

Bush prizes personal loyalty above all. The decades of his political career have been undistinguished: serving for short terms in sensitive or troubled government agencies (the CIA, the U.N., the Embassy in China) whenever an uncontroversial interim head was needed; picked by Reagan to be Vice-President because no one could possibly object; spending his eight years in the position only visible at state funerals. He loyally served his superiors, modifying whatever values he had to conform with theirs. (Bush, it is now forgotten, was once considered to be a "liberal" Republican. In the days before birth control was revealed to Protestants to be the work of Satan, he had even served on the board of the Texas Planned Parenthood.) Now that he's the boss, he, in turn, demands absolute loyalty from his inferiors. His selection of Dan Quayle was a perfect example: a lump of cerebral anti-matter from which Bush may expect never to experience the slightest deviation. (Asked, in the campaign, why he wanted to be Vice-President, Quayle replied: "It seems like a good career move.")

Noriega, Bush's ward from his CIA days, though hardly the incarnation of evil as he has been portrayed here, is indeed the essence of betrayal. For years he played both lucrative sides of every fence: collecting a salary from the Drug Enforcement Agency while helping the Medellín cartel, working for the CIA and making deals with Castro, arming the *contras* and shipping American parts to the Sandinistas. (The only surprising thing about Noriega is that he never offered to both shelter and assassinate Salman Rushdie.) This was clearly more than Bush could stand. According to his Texan wisdom, if you don't lasso a rogue bull, the whole herd will go crazy. With Noriega on the loose, Panama was becoming too unpredictable— in a sense, too Panamanian for American taste.

The invasion was an enormous political gamble, and I, for one, would never have imagined its astonishing success: Bush, according to the latest polls, is now the most popular President after one year in office since John Kennedy. This, for a mildly unpleasant man whose normal speech is idiosyncratic to the point of incommunicability. (Visiting Auschwitz in 1987, he remarked, "Boy, they were big on crematoriums, weren't they?") This, after Henry Kissinger's remark during the campaign that George Bush would lose even if he ran against himself, and after having been elected by only 55% of the 50% who bothered to vote. This, for a man who had spent his first day as President showing everyone in the office a calculator that squirts water.

Part of this success is due to the media coverage, which, speaking of loyalty, blew bugles for the troops with the ardor of Gunga Din. Here, from *The Boston Globe*, is a sample of the kind of news reports Americans were reading:

In this city's poorest neighborhoods, artillery shells and machine gun fire leveled the homes of the poorest inhabitants and destroyed the meager possessions of thousands, but it lifted their spirits and gave them hope.

Across this devastated and emotionally and economically exhausted urban war zone, people stood amid the ruins yes-

106

terday shedding tears of happiness in spite of their predicament and cheering the Americans whose weapons turned many of their homes into smoldering ruins.

"Thank you, President Boosh! Thank you, President Boosh!" exulted Alejandro Bullen as he stood shirtless not twenty yards from the still-smoking rubble of the apartment building where he once lived.

Night after night, the television news told us about the twenty-six American soldiers who had died, but never mentioned the Panamanian civilians, although it was obvious that whole neighborhoods had been devastated. Night after night, we were regaled with stories of Noriega's pornographic magazines which, according to the Pentagon, had shocked the soldiers who captured his house (being, as they were, more accustomed to reading *Being and Nothingness* around the barracks), of his red underwear to ward off the evil eye (where was that evil eye looking?), of the fifty pounds which became fifty kilos of cocaine in his freezer (which, weeks later, were revealed to be tamales— another form of addiction), and of the heavy-metal music blasting into the Vatican Nuncio to drive the opera-loving Noriega (not to mention the presumably Gregorian chant-loving priests) mad. Not once did we hear that Bush had killed more Panamanians than anyone— certainly not Noriega— since its 1899 war with Colombia. Not once was the evil Panama of Noriega— who killed a few dozen enemies and had less than a hundred political prisoners— compared with the mass slaughters by our allies in El Salvador and Guatemala. Only rarely was it revealed that the rest of the world— even Maggie of the Malvinas— was aghast.

The narcissism of the Panama palindrome cannot be attributed merely to nationalism, a last fit of fervor from a waning superpower, or racism. (Though anti-Hispanic feeling, particularly in the "sunbelt" states, is rising faster than the Hispanic population. Its most genteel battleground is the movement to have English declared the national language— which is based on the assumption that the Anglos are able to speak it.) No, the real source of Panamania can be summed up in one word: drugs.

Thanks again to television— the true "unacknowledged legislator of the world"— a national problem has been transformed into a national panic. Drugs have become an Evil emanating with the power of a million Noriegas. Their use escalated enormously during the Reagan years, and the populace has been made to feel helpless before this monster and its children: violent street criminals, crazed teenagers, babies born addicted. These days, every time one turns on the television one is pummeled by yet another horror story.

Very little is said about the causes of this epidemic, though it is obvious why, in the 1980's, millions of Americans found it necessary to turn their brains into refried beans. Reagan devastated the poor: two or three million became homeless (one-third of them children) and unemployment for blacks, Hispanics and poor whites remains phenomenally high. There is little else to do in the ghetto but smoke crack, which is cheap, and drug-dealing is the only guaranteed (and lucrative) job. The middle class has become poor— families with both parents working cannot possibly enjoy the kind of lives they led in the 1960's and 1970's— and drugs and television are its main forms of relief. And, at the top of the heap, the frenetic greed of the corporate raiders and free-ranging entrepreneurs who flourished under Reagan was fueled by the sensations of speed and omnipotence given them by an epic of cocaine lines which, in the beginning, only they could afford.

Rather than address the social problems that have created this mass addiction, Reagan declared a rhetorical war. (Meanwhile, drug prices crashed from the glut on the market, including a 75% drop in the wholesale price of cocaine.) And now Bush seems to be turning that rhetoric into action, of which Panama may be only the first salvo.

There is, as there always is, a hidden agenda to this drug war. As everyone outside of Washington knows, the Cold War ended in 1989. [For me, evidence that the world had changed was visible locally in December 1988, when Gorbachev visited New York: the huge neon billboard in Times Square was flashing a hammer and sickle as the crowds along Broadway chanted, "Gorby! Gorby!"] Even *Time* magazine which, under Henry Luce, was the preeminent journalistic flank of the Cold War and practically the architect of our policy toward China (thanks to Luce's friendship with Chiang Kai-shek, fostered by the Catholic Church)—a policy that not only refused to recognize a quarter of humanity, but created the wars in Korea and Indochina to "contain" the Yellow/Red Menace— even *Time* was now writing:

Scenarios for a Soviet invasion of Western Europe have always had a touch of paranoid fantasy about them. A new consensus is emerging, that the Soviet threat is not what it used to be. The real point, however, is that it never was. The doves in the Great Debate of the past forty years were right all along.

With *Time* on their coffee tables, Americans are slowly realizing that the country ruined itself fighting a war that never existed. Though the mirror situation is, of course, far worse in the Soviet

Union, the U.S has the worst health, education, transportation, and social services of any Western nation, and a swamp of environmental problems— while, in the Reagan-Bush years, two-thirds of every tax dollar went to war, though no official wars were actually being fought. Even superhawks like Robert McNamara (the Secretary of Defense during the Vietnam War) are now saying that the Pentagon budget could be cut in half overnight with no effect to our "defense."

Sentiments like these have caused a panic in Washington. Our foreign policy— which, for decades, could be summed up in one sentence: Any enemy of our enemy is our friend— is in a shambles. Bush, an old soldier who still checks for Communists under his bed, has lapsed into catatonia before the events in Eastern Europe, standing still amidst a stampede of capitalists rushing in. [Bush calls this "prudence," but there may be another story: The far right seriously believes that *glasnost* is the ultimate Soviet plot. By pretending to declare peace, Gorbachev will effect the disbandment of NATO, withdrawal of American troops from Europe and drastic reductions in Western military strength— at which point the Soviets will march in and finally conquer the world! If it seems far-fetched that any "responsible" leaders would believe this, let us remember that the Vice-President idolizes his father, a founder, in the 1950's, of the John Birch Society, which thought that Eisenhower was a KGB agent and the fluoridation of water a Communist plot, and who is now associated with a magazine that claims that the Democrats are controlled directly by Moscow, and the Republicans by Trotskyites in Tel Aviv.]

The Pentagon, faced with hippie flower children in the Politburo, is quivering in its spit-polished boots. For the military to hold on to its hardware, and for America to continue to run on a war economy, obviously a new enemy had to be found, and quickly. That enemy is drugs— a concept more concrete in its particulars, but, as an alien force, equally abstract as Communism. So the Drug War is on, and the country is cheering.

Domestically, Bush and his minions are calling for more police, more courts and more prisons. (Prisons— unlike schools, hospitals or museums— being the only public buildings Republicans like to construct.) And within the Pentagon, according to military journals, those who see the Drug War as the only means of self-preservation, given the world situation, are prevailing over those reluctant to become mired in another Vietnam-style jungle war. (In, for example, Peru, where the Sendero Luminoso— real Communists!—is in alliance with the coca growers and controls vast areas of the country, where the Peruvian Army is fighting a losing battle, and where Green Beret military "advisers" are already in place. Like Panama, it's the perfect spot to simultaneously "restore democracy" and "stop the flow of drugs at their source.")

All of this will, needless to say, do nothing to stop drugs. Drugs are the ideal capitalist venture: the market is limitless, anyone can get into the business, and, with very little money and hard work, make a fortune. And, as Eastern Europe has demonstrated, people will stop at nothing to get the consumer products they want, be it blue jeans or cocaine. For every hundred dealers the Drug War eliminates, a thousand will take their place. It is, after arms dealing, the second-largest business in the world, and one that requires far less capital and expertise.

The extraordinary success of the Panama invasion has made the prospects for a post-Cold War peace in the 1990's seem dubious. Right now, Bush is standing on the mountain of his popularity, scanning the horizon with his binoculars for new territory to conquer.

111

....

NOTES FOR *SULFUR* III

[*Written for the back pages of* Sulfur, *1990-1991.*]

....

The NEA

I was cheered by the news this morning that the head of some Boston nut-group had condemned the opening there of the Mapplethorpe show as "avant-garde, anti-Christian, anti-American, and perverse." The irony of the current NEA controversy is that these Soldiers of God may indeed effect a Confucian rectification of names: restoring the term "avant-garde" to its former place of dignity as subverter of norms.

Day after day, defenders of the NEA piously repeat that these works are not obscene, but Art that Enriches the Human Soul. It's not true. They are, like all art, obscene: presenting, literally, an *opposite scene*, opposite to the world that is before our eyes.

We should be emphasizing that the primary function of art is subversion: the bringing to light of the sub(terranean) versions: the versions that reveal that the world is not quite what we thought it is.

112

There has been only one reason for the perennial suppression of art: it tells you what you don't know, and that's more than most states can stand.

It should be remembered that the NEA is a product of the Vietnam War, the moment in this century when American artists and writers were most visibly the enemies of the state. It was founded and then expanded by our two wiliest presidents, Johnson and Nixon. They sure knew what they were doing. Snip through all the rhetoric of how *my* art could never be compromised by a government grant and one fact is plain: Through the Reagan years, the century's most shameful period in American history, the artists were silent. We will need a new generation to bury this generation of good Germans.

Parallel to this was the universities' friendly takeover of student protest by introducing "relevancy" to the curriculum: teaching what the students already knew, showing their sensitivity to student expression by encouraging workshops in various forms of "creativity." This required, of course, the wholesale importation of writers and artists, and the hitherto unimaginable invention of "poet" as a comfortable middle-class career. With it came a kind of collective amnesia: no one seems to remember that, before 1970, the university was considered the enemy of contemporary poetry.

I remember laughing, in the early 1980's, when I saw the Norton Critical Edition of *On the Road*, alongside *The Scarlet Letter* and *Billy Budd*: it had taken less than thirty years to entomb that once-scandalous book. Today the leap from the barricades to the marble halls is nearly instantaneous. Last night's bad boy or girl of the arts this morning receives a hefty fellowship, a university chair, a museum retrospective, a shelf of critical exegesis. We're kidding ourselves if we think that this is a sign of a healthy plurality in the institutions— which can, and should, only function as monuments to the dead— or that this hasn't changed the face of the arts.

Is it more incredible that Karen Finley's NEA grant was over-ruled, or that someone who publicly shoves yams up her ass should dutifully fill out the endless government forms to attest to her craft? That this and the other NEA cases have been generally condemned as "censorship"—here at the end of a century that murdered and still murders thousands of artists and writers, banned and still bans tens of thousands of works— is indicative of how cozy and drowsy the American arts have become.

Nearly everything of enduring interest produced in the last 150 years was made by the perverse, the obscene, the ostracized, the subversive. These days I find myself nearly alone in hoping that the right will succeed in making the arts perverse again. Not so long ago, the goal of artists and writers was to work in such a way that no one would dream of giving you money for it.

....

T.S. Eliot

T his morning I also happened to be reading (in Wayne Koestenbaum's *Double Talk: The Erotics of Male Literary Collaboration*) this anecdote of our pillar of rectitude, T.S. Eliot:

Conrad Aiken had praised Eliot's 1925 *Poems*. Eliot replied by sending him a page ripped out of *The Midwives' Gazette* in which he had underlined a description of vaginal discharge: "*blood, mucous, and shreds of mucous... purulent offensive discharge.*" Aiken at the time was in the hospital suffering from an anal fistula. In the accompanying letter, Eliot wrote: "Have you tried Kotex for it... KOTEX. Used with success by Blue-eyed Claude the Cabin Boy." The reference was to that perennial frat-boy favorite, "The Good Ship Venus," to which Eliot had written some additional lyrics, which he enclosed. Claude was: "a clever little nipper/ who filled his ass with broken glass/ and circumcised the skipper."

....

Mary Oppen

The recent death of Mary Oppen sent me back to her autobiography *Meaning A Life* (Black Sparrow). Too few know it: a classic of "objectivist" prose. In her poetry Mary often sounded like George; in the prose however she reveals herself as Reznikoff's worthiest disciple. It is extraordinary how much she was able to pack into the simplest declarative sentence. Equally remarkable, at any given moment in the book the lives of Mary and George— and Mary's emotional responses— are unfolding amidst the enormous events in the world. This is not so much a modernist collage as the result of modernist collage. A 20th century sensibility: the news as autobiography.

[1990]

Barbaric Lyricism

In the last issue of *Sulfur*, my untitled article on the poets of Baghdad [reprinted as "The City of Peace" in *Outside Stories*] was preceded by a quote from Whitman under the title "Barbaric Lyricism." Some thought this the title and epigraph to my piece. It wasn't, and it's especially unfortunate to have "barbaric" attached to it, when the point was to debarbarize, if only a little, the place.

For barbaric lyricism, or lyric barbarism, there was the "Victory" parade in New York the other day, celebrating the slaughter of 200,000 people, the displacement of five million more, the "apocalyptic" leveling of a small country, the tens of thousands of future deaths from disease and starvation, and at least a decade of ecological calamity. A Patriot missile was gar-landed like a Shiva lingam and paraded up Broadway; in the evening, the local pyrotechnic geniuses, the Gruccis, recreated the effect of a Patriot hitting a Scud over the Statue of Liberty, to the theme from "Star Wars."

George Plimpton and the *Paris Review* seized the moment for a fund-raising "Spring Revel" at $150 a head featuring "Dinner and Huge Fireworks Show Celebrating the Return of the Troops" aboard a hired yacht. The "Revel" committee included William Styron, Kurt Vonnegut, William Kennedy, Peter Mathiessen, Frances Fitzgerald, Norman Mailer and E.L. Doctorow, among other stars of the American "left." Said Plimpton to the *Village Voice*: "There's no political statement in this at all." Said Fitzger-ald: "Things are going to happen anyway. If it's going on out

116

there, why miss it?" Said Styron: "I don't think it's incongruous, being against the war in principle and feeling that the troops deserve a cheer."

....

Olson and Rexroth Biographies

In America, where tens of millions live alone and most people move every three years, where they rarely see their relatives, and where Main Street has been replaced by the strip and the mall, hardly anyone knows anyone any more. Or more exactly: people mainly know, and know best, the people they don't know: celebrities. The village has indeed become a global village, but that global village is Hollywood. What is the Johnny Carson Show, for example, but an amiable evening on the front porch dishing the neighbors? Even better, it is a village where the neighbors stay the same, unlike one's actual neighbors. The stable presence of their unstable lives is not only a source of daily news and developments, it is a subject— probably the only safe subject— to talk about with the local strangers.

The language of the tribe is gossip, and in perpetual, individual diaspora the need for gossip becomes insatiable. In lives where mainly nothing happens except television, and where television wildly exaggerates the danger in something, anything, happening, there is a craving for "real life"—not to live it, but to watch it. Sensationalist "news" programs, "true" crime stories, the afternoon talk shows, funny or pornographic amateur home videos:

packaged real life is inevitably weird, and getting weirder. Into the safety of one's own bunker comes the mesmerizing news that what was suspected is true: the boy and girl next door— those real people— really are freaks.

And so is everyone else we've ever heard about, but don't know. It is a Puritan legacy, the tale of the life of sin: only England and America produce biographies in bulk, and in America they are poring out every day with their emphasized bad news, bizarre and sad stories. It now seems that a life— any life, yours or mine— examined by someone else is not worth living.

This biographical imperative cuts across the strata of taste. There is even a market— or they would not be published— for biographies of contemporary poets, preferably dead, which inevitably seem to issue from houses that never would have considered publishing the poet's work.

The latest, released in the same week by W.W. Norton, are Linda Hamalian's *A Life of Kenneth Rexroth* and Tom Clark's *Charles Olson: The Allegory of a Poet's Life*. Both are about 400 pages long, and both wave the Bad Boy banner with covers showing their subjects not typing but engaged in what current American mores now consider to be self-destructive hedonism: smoking.

Hamalian's is by far the better book. Rexroth's life can only be compared, among the American poets, with Pound or Langston Hughes for its variety and frantic pace. Hamalian— who interviewed hundreds of his friends and enemies— needs every one of her apparently allotted 400 pages just to keep up. (I've been told that another 200 pages, dealing with the work, were cut.) The book's impossible to put down as it zips through the chronology past the factual trees. Yet I suspect its ultimate value will be, years from now, as the groundwork for the multi-volume *Life and Times*, on the order of Painter or Edel, that Rexroth deserves.

Clark, on the other hand, relies mainly on published sources and interviews with some mutual friends, like Ed Dorn. And Olson, with the exceptions of his time as a Democratic Party flack and at Black Mountain, spent most of his life first not writing and then writing. This gives Clark plenty of room for rumination on the work, none of it particularly illuminating. His one coup, perhaps worth reading the book, is the previously little-known story of, and unpublished correspondence with, Frances Boldereff.

[In brief: At age 39, Olson is still floundering, has written little and published less. He gets a letter out of the blue from a woman in a small town in Pennsylvania telling him he's a genius. The correspondence accelerates to the rate of two or three letters a day. Boldereff sends him into various branches of arcana that become part of the Olson canon; phrases from both their letters become embedded in the poems he's suddenly furiously writing. Almost a year later they meet for the first time, Olson's first weekend of passion. (As Clark typically tells us— and how does he know?—Olson was tormented that his penis wasn't as Maximus as the rest of him.) Olson, however, won't leave his wife, and for many years the pattern of frenetic letters and rare passionate meetings continues.]

Hamalian clearly starts off as an acolyte, but the deeper she gets into Rexroth's incessant philandering, paranoia, and abuse of women, her disdain grows. [Rexroth, the promoter of many women poets, was a personal misogynist; Olson, which is worse, an ideological one. Both books indulge in retrospective moralizing, yet it is curious that both men were surrounded by women who deified them, even after they had found the men impossible to live with. Connie Olson, after one of many separations, says she doesn't believe in God, because Charles is her God. Rexroth's second wife is the godmother of the daughter, named after the first wife, who is born to his third wife, to whom he's bigamously married. And so on.]

Clark apparently began with the image of a pathetic, tormented genius, and then piled on the evidence; there's no sense of Olson's charisma. And a pall hangs over his book from his willful, criminal neglect of George Butterick— who is mentioned only three times in passing as one of the disciples. Clark ends with Olson's funeral, as Olson did not: *Sulfur* readers need hardly be told that nearly everything we know about Olson, the texts of most of the poems and much of the prose, critical glosses of thousands of references, and the very existence of the third volume of *Maximus*— the volume that is, for me, his great work— is due entirely to Butterick. Clark, whatever his motives, has written a biography of Kafka without Max Brod.

Two lives that couldn't be more different: Rexroth the adventurer, Olson the bookworm. Rexroth the cosmopolitan, Olson the local hick. Rexroth the Don Juan, Olson the timid. Rexroth in the American wilderness, Olson obsessively researching the West for years before actually going out to see it. Rexroth the Buddhist and Christian, deep in the selflessness of ritual and meditation, Olson the Jungian, deep in the symbols of self. Rexroth compulsively surrounded by people of all types, Olson by a few disciples and, in the last years, living alone in an apartment piled with trash where the phone never rang, writing on every available surface, even the walls, sleeping all day and wandering empty streets at night. For the life of an American poet, it is Rexroth's that is the more incredible.

Most incredible now, when he is remembered but largely unread, is that Rexroth was— alone with Hughes, and Pound in

120

the teens and twenties— an American poet who was a public intellectual figure, famous among general readers. (Ginsberg's celebrity is another matter.) His public exposure in the fifties and sixties seems unimaginable for an American poet today: a weekly radio show, a twice-weekly column in the *San Francisco Examiner*, book reviews or articles once a month in *The Nation* and four or five times a year in the *N.Y. Times Book Review*, the twice-monthly "Classics Revisited" series in the *Saturday Review*, further articles in magazines from *Art News* to *Mademoiselle* and *Nugget* (whatever happened to *Nugget*?), records of his poetry readings, sales of 10,000 for a new book of poems and 100,000 for the Chinese translations, interviews in the national media, even talk of a television show — plus the endless local discussion groups and readings he organized. Rexroth, in other words, led the life generally available to a poet nearly everywhere except in America.

Olson, however, led a more normal American poet's life. He died with most of his work unpublished, and most of the rest out of print. He spoke grandly to his "fellow citizens" of the "Republic of Letters," but had only a few devout followers. He planned national and international institutions and symposia and think tanks to get the message out, all of which came to nothing. There is a sad moment in the letters to Corman where he compares *Origin* magazine, with its print run of 300— as he had once compared the few remaining students at Black Mountain— to Mao's band in the Yenan caves.

Finally, it is true that few among us could survive the investigation of a biographer and not emerge a monster. Taking out the garbage is not the stuff of biographies, the garbage itself is: the petty cruelties, the hypocrisies revealed in the archives of correspondence, the mistakes and indiscretions, the bad days, bad habits, bad blood.

But the deeper question is what the biography of a poet does to subsequent readings of the work. It cannot help but localize the poem, cheapen it, fix it permanently in its biographical interpretation. So now we know that among Pound's last words, the great lines "When one's friends hate each other/ how can there be peace in the world?" refers to the bickering among three women in his harem. So now we know that Rexroth, the century's great celebrant of married love was, simultaneous to those poems, writing mash-notes to half-a-dozen other women. So now we know who Frank Moore is, and why Olson wondered. (In a letter to Ferrini in the first *Origin* he had revealed what's buried behind Lufkin's diner.) Is "The Librarian"—and the most mysterious lines in American poetry— ruined? And what happened to his own reading of the lines, from writing them (when he's clearly talking to himself) to publishing them (when he must consider their effect)? Frank Moore troubles my insomnia.

....

Future PMLA *article*

The signature Olson syntax— the dangling participles which Creeley picks up, and the sudden exclamations— always seemed to come from nowhere, certainly not Massachusetts. Then the other day it struck me: Hopkins. One of many examples:

...My heart in hiding
  Stirred for a bird, — the achieve of, the mastery
   of the thing!

The paradox is, the Figure of Outward, the poet of projection, nearly always reads like an escaping convict with only one leg.

....

Persuasive New Defense of Traditional Prosody

*P*rosody remains embedded in *the finished work...[like] the armature in a statue: an essential part of the finished structure. We do not judge a statue by its armature, any more than we judge a beauty contest by the X-rays of the competitors. But what the X-rays show is essential to beauty; without the armature of the skeleton Miss America or Mr. Universe would collapse to a heap of flab..."*

  —John Frederick Nims, *The Six-Cornered Snowflake.*
             [1991]

....

READING POETRY

[Written for a panel on "Poetry & Knowledge"
at St. Mark's Church, New York, 1990.]

I've read it every day of my life since I was thirteen. It is, among the man-made artifacts, my primary source of knowledge of the stuff of this world and the next. Its limitless archive of tiny and piercing, vast and enveloping perceptions of "the way things work and move" (Keats) has forever altered and continually alters my own. It is my religion, in as much as it is an affirmation of the sacrality of all things; it brings me news from the unknown, beyond my imagination; it is a daily opportunity to talk with the dead. Bursting into sound, running through its cycles of silence and sound, ending as silence: a poem is the Hindu history of the universe.

But poetry is also— and this is rarely, if ever, said— a source of knowledge at its most literal: information. My life with poetry began when I discovered that it was talking about the same things— and not only emotional things— that interested me: I was thirteen, wanted to be an archeologist, at that moment reading everything I could find on pre-Columbian Mesoamerica in an unusually good high school library. Stuck inside some fat book— Prescott or Bernal Díaz on the Conquest— was the pamphlet of Octavio Paz's *Sun Stone*, in Muriel Rukeyser's translation. It was

124

the first modern poem I'd come across, and more, it was—unimaginable for me until then— both a *use* of the ancient (in this case, the Aztec calendar) to read the contemporary (20th century history and one man's autobiography) and a recreation of it in an intensely musical language. A boy's discovery that poetry— this language that didn't sound like anything else— was a doorway opening onto all times and all places.

From there I wandered undirected through the poetry shelves, poets— my real teachers, not the bored dictators of the classrooms— leading me from one poet to another. But, equally important, poets and poems were taking me into worlds besides literature. In those adolescent years— to take a few examples— I first began reading about Buddhism because of *The Waste Land*, which simultaneously sent me into the Grail and medieval mythology. Lorca took me to books on the Spanish Civil War; Hart Crane to Columbus' diaries and 19th century New York and Atlantis; Williams to colonial America; Pound to Renaissance Italy and the history of China (and later to Chinese itself) and the Anglo-Saxons and medieval Provence; Olson to the Delphic Oracle and the pre-Socratics, to Mesopotamia, to the whaleship chronicles and the history of agriculture; Artaud to the Tarahumaras and the Black Death. The list is endless, and still continues: hardly any of the books I know cannot ultimately be traced to a poem or poet.

Similarly, most of my travels started out from poems, beginning at sixteen when Neruda's *Canto General* sent me off to Machu Picchu and the Atacama Desert. The places I now happen to know best, beyond the great metropolises, were first literary landscapes: India and Mexico in Paz, Provence in the troubadours, Italy in Dante and Pound. And the cities themselves live for me as a simultaneous moment of the poets walking their streets and as a collage of their paper monuments. Conversely, to read poetry is to be alive in the city: the modern poem *is* a city, even when its ostensible subject is the wilderness.

I confess I adhere to the 19th century image of each poem existing as part of a glittering net of correspondences. I've never understood the concept of the discrete literary artifact, imagined by the New Critics as a golden bowl (or was it a well-wrought urn?) or elaborated by the so-called post-moderns as some sort of textual outer space debris, alone and floating nowhere. For me, any poem worth reading always goes somewhere, as its descriptive language implies (verse, metaphor, metrical feet), always is somewhere.

In countless oral stories the hunter, tracking a certain prey, follows an unrepeatable path into another world. It is the origin of the "way," in its universal religious sense. Nearly all my intellectual and physical wanderings have been on the track of poems. Naturally many other things might have taken me on similar paths, but poetry happened to be my totemic animal. And strangely, these zillion bits of the world were learned from what is traditionally considered to be the most rarefied, unworldly world of writing.

ROTHENBERG: NEW YORK / 1968

[*Written for the book,* Joy! Praise! Jerome Rothenberg at 60, *edited by Pierre Joris (Ta'awil Books), 1991.*]

Zero birthdays are an occasion when it's forgivable to drag out the old photos, and there's one snapshot I want to pull from the overstuffed Rothenberg album: an important early moment in his work and, it has turned out, an indelible one in my life: the publication of *Technicians of the Sacred.*

I had twigged to Jerry as an adolescent in the mid-60's: *Some/Thing* magazine, the "rituals" at Judson Church and the Something Else pamphlet *Ritual* (1966), the first JR book I remember buying. He was already on my map when we first met in 1967 at the elaborate parties surrounding the London Poetry Festival— a century ago— I, a teenage nerd following the hors d'oeuvres trays through a crowd of grandmasters (Olson, Neruda, Paz, MacDiarmid, Ungaretti) poetry stars (Auden, Spender, Berryman, Empson— who had silenced the room with a shout: "No one insults my wife's boyfriend!") pop icons (Ginsberg, Burroughs, Trocchi, Mick Jagger, Marianne Faithfull) and hundreds of rising or failing practitioners, many of them now ghosts. Jerry's *Between* had just come out from Fulcrum; there I had finally caught up with *The Seven Hells of the Jigoku Zoshi*, the first of the JR medium-length sequences, and still lively, though now more likely to be read as an arrow pointing directly to his masterpiece, *Khurbn*.

There were, in the later 60's, two New York Schools. The first, of course, from the Donald Allen taxonomy: Ashbery, O'Hara, Koch, Guest, Schuyler, and others, and the "second generation" of Berrigan, Waldman, Padgett, and so many more. But there was also "my" N.Y. School— mine as a reader— a group as coherent as any poetry group, but too young for the *New American Poets* and, in retrospect, whose individual reputations perhaps suffered from the lack of a name, a compartment in the brain to locate them in the subsequent population explosion: Rothenberg, Antin, Eshleman, Kelly, Economou, Owens, Schwerner, Wakoski, MacLow and others, with Paul Blackburn, in terms of publication, an older brother.

Both came, in part, out of Surrealism. The official N.Y. School from certain aspects of the French poems: irony, wit, whimsical juxtaposition, random apprehensions of ordinary life, the panorama of the street. The "others" from Surrealism's exoticism and the exotic branches of the movement itself, from its politics (as response to one war and prophecy of another), preoccupation with the magical power of the "primitive," and techniques like chance operations, writing under hallucinogenic drugs, collage, and performance. The difference, say, between the poems of Péret and Péret as translator of the *Popol Vuh*, strange dreams and prophetic dreams, Roussel in Africa and Artaud in Mexico, DeChirico and Duchamp.

I had picked up on JR early because my image of poetry was (still is) as the place where one got the news from abroad, from the dead, and from the gods. With the first page of the first issue of *Some/Thing*, JR's "workings" from the *Florentine Codex*, I knew that this was part of(MacDiarmid's words) "the kind of poetry I want." The book I eagerly awaited, and then devoured when it finally came out in 1968, was *Technicians of the Sacred*.

1968: a tired story we tell over and over, the Great War for which we are the old soldiers: the year of the international student revolutions, the assassinations, the conviction that the entire world was on the verge of radical transformation, from the structure of society and state to the details of body ornament. But more: the belief that the way to the new was the old: hallucinogens as the source of ancient wisdom, tribal communism as the answer to capitalism, the wilderness to industrialization; an "Electric Tibet."

A year of continual unforeseeable developments in the day's papers, and an equally incredible poring out of news from the poetry presses. Alongside *Technicians*, these were some of the new books appearing like oracles that year: Pound's *Drafts and Fragments*, Bunting's *Collected Poems*, Oppen's *Of Being Numerous*, the second volume of Olson's *Maximus* and the first available edition of the *Mayan Letters*, Duncan's *Bending the Bow*, Snyder's *The Back Country*, Rexroth's *Collected Longer Poems* and his translations of Reverdy, Niedecker's *North Central*, Eshleman's translation of Vallejo's *Human Poems*, Blackburn's *In. On. or About the Premises*, MacLow's *22 Light Poems*, Enzensberger's *Poems for People Who Don't Read Poetry* (translated by Jerry with Michael Hamburger), Ginsberg's *Planet News*, Dorn's *Gunslinger I*... as well as small books and pamphlets by many others (including two by Rothenberg), *Caterpillar* magazine, *"A"* serialized in *Poetry*, countless readings against the war, the populist readings and jazz collaborations of the black poets— and the first word from Don Juan! Nothing more tedious than the joys of someone else's youth, and yet: it is a moment from which I, then 19, like so many others, never recovered.

It was a moment when the world and poetry-world were inextricable, and both were devoted to political change, passionate commitment, commitment to passion, alternate realities, the foreign and the ancient. *Technicians*, more than an anthology of tribal and oral poetries— like Willard Trask's two-volume *The Unwritten Song*, which had just appeared in 1966 and 1967 and had gone unnoticed— was an attempt to bring it all together, the "rite of participation" invoked the year before by Duncan in *Caterpillar*, the true coming of Here Comes Everybody.

It is incredible how many of those everybodies Rothenberg would go on to embody. Here, among his friends, it needs no reiteration. Only this: he is probably the gateway to more corners of the earth than any poet in this century. In the pages of a Rothenberg book— the poems as much as the anthologies— the world has a coherence. Perhaps this coherence is false— the tangle of correspondences from Altaic shamans to Blake to Kabbalah to Mixtec codices to East Village performances— but we cannot deny that Rothenberg, as so few others, has managed to construct a world. And more: it is a world, even in the hells of *Khurbn*, of ecstasy and a fundamental joy. Not Utopia, but a model of the world to set against the world.

Startling that, at 60, Jerry enters the ranks of the senior poets, alongside the equally suddenly venerable Creeley, Snyder, Ashbery, Tarn and Ginsberg, and next year, Antin. Yet his 60 is a youthfulness the lugubrious youths of poetry-world might well emulate. Who among them has as many projects cooking? And who among us, the now incomprehensibly middle-aged, has the curiosity and erudition, the Cinemascope frame and the genuine multiculturalism, the enthusiasm, the accomplishments that Rothenberg had at 40?

To put it simply: I have read everything that Jerry has written, translated or edited, and I still read it all the time. He is the rare poet whose last book is his best book, and whose next book I'll read the day I get it. At this moment of the breaking-up of nations and the end of the ideologies, the disaster and threat of the next decade and the next century will be ethnocentricity, nationalism, all the forms of excluding the other. Ethnopoetics— a poetics not of "the people," but of "peoples"— could be one of the ways out. American poets, in worse isolation than ever, symptomatic of the times, have stopped talking to strangers, stopped listening to the news from elsewhere. Think of what informed those Greatest Hits of 1968 and what informs even the Hits of 1991. Ethnopoetics was this great pod exploding, but the seeds still lie dormant. Now that the 25-year time-lag of recognition (Pound's Law) is nearly over, I think— maybe I'm crazy— that the moment for a revitalization, a new generation of ethnopoetics, is almost here. And with it, the realization that Rothenberg, all along, has been one of the wisest in the tribe, and the one who, amidst general indifference, has been taking care of the sacred bundles.

....

TALKING ON DRUGS

[*A conversation in Mexico with Magali Tercero and Roberto Tejada*
for an issue of La Jornada Semanal *devoted to "Intellectuals and Drugs,"*
1992. Translated from the Spanish.]

To begin with, I should say that, as a loyal member of the generation of '68— one who still sleeps in his uniform— I was naturally involved with drugs and hallucinogens. But I should also say, for certain elements of this newspaper's readership, that it's now twenty-odd years later... There are two aspects to this: one I'll speak of as a writer, and the other as a teenaged inhabitant of the United States at the end of the 1960's.

As I writer, I think that the experience of hallucinogenic drugs can be useful because under their effect ordinary objects are transformed: the chair you are sitting in is more than a chair; it is a chair that has its own aura of signification. It is a way of discovering that the world is not what it seems, and moreover that there is another world that can be explored. But this is only a first step, because one goes from there to the discovery that in poetry the world is transformed in exactly the same way as on drugs: In a poem a chair is not a chair. It is a chair charged with meaning. As soon as one makes this discovery, drugs become unnecessary.

But I also happen to believe that the origin of writing— more specifically, when writing goes beyond the act of tallying— is in hallucinogenic drugs. One of the experiences of drugs is that it creates a correspondence between abstract signs and meaning. Under its effects one can look at cloud formations or animal tracks or tree branches against the sky and find significance. In fact, many cultures have myths in which the origin of writing is tied to hallucinogens. For example, it is extremely interesting that the Mazatec shaman, María Sabina, who was illiterate, said that, when under the influence of the mushrooms, she received a book from which she "read" her healing songs. And the Mexican codices were, in part, mnemonic devices that perhaps were read— or could only be read— after taking mushrooms or other hallucinogens, or after having performed other actions that produced hallucinations, like the bloodletting practiced by the Maya. Under the influence of drugs the images of the codices would have taken on meaning. No doubt these books were not for the general public, but were exclusively for an intellectual or priestly elite. Yet they represent that small leap from abstract signs taking on a personal significance under drugs to abstract signs having a shared significance— in other words, reading.

On the other side, in the 60's taking drugs was a political act because it was an act, however futile, against the established order, and a negation of the prevailing reality.

We were looking for an alternate reality because we rightfully couldn't stand the existing reality, which meant primarily the Vietnam War, the most visible and clearly unjust of the world's injustices at that moment. And the other reality that we were discovering was, of course, a spiritual reality. Spiritual reality is always the enemy of political reality; the way the two have been reconciled historically has been through the institutionalization of religion.

All of the religions have begun as a revolt against the established order: Jesus or Mahavira or the Buddha were dangerous people. The way to weaken that danger was to institutionalize their teachings and develop stricter ties between the social and religious orders. Thus the counterculture was a kind of return to the origins of religion— in a certain sense— and with it a return to human origins. This naturally led to a fascination, in the 60's, with American Indians. There was the inevitable identification with an imagined "simple" and communal life, close to nature and the gods, that had been obliterated by technology and capitalist greed. It was said then, romantically, that the "Woodstock nation" was like the Sioux nation, something one carried on one's back. Coincident to the "baby boom," the 50's existentialist alienated outsider— the survivor of the Second World War— had now expanded into a group of internal exiles with communal yearnings, a "band of outsiders" as Godard's movie was called.

Taking drugs was inseparable from what was happening at that moment, from the demonstrations against the Vietnam War to rock music, communes, the return to the land, and so on. All of this was of one piece— the counterculture was a whole culture— and can't be broken down. That is to say, we took drugs much in the same way that our parents went to work.

This makes it difficult, I think, for members of my generation to have too much interest in the drug-taking among those who followed us. In the 90's it has become a form of entertainment, a sort of MTV OF the mind. If you take drugs you're of course opposing your parents; if you take drugs too much you're opposing yourself; but you're not, in any way, opposing society.

Why did the spiritual quests of the 60's seem, in the end, to have lead nowhere?

Basically what happened was the McDonaldization of the counterculture, exactly as it had occurred with Beat culture. Everything that was considered radical in the 60's turned into popular consumer choices: rock music, marijuana, exotic cuisine, comfortable work clothes, long hair, the "natural look" for women, vegetarianism, sex without marriage, etc. Look at the Beats in the 50's, as they are represented, say, in Kerouac's novels. Yesterday's wildness is today's conventionality: red wine, Chinese food eaten with chopsticks, jazz, and so on. And the ideology behind these material manifestations takes another form and becomes part of another culture, or it merely fades away.

Sixties' youth genuinely believed that the world was on the verge of a radical change. It seems absurd now, but that was what it was like. We thought that the other reality would replace the existing reality— and for this reason the counterculture was more than adolescent rebellion, it was a genuine belief that in a few short years the dominant culture was going to be transformed. (I'll never forget those alarmed articles in *Time* magazine: "Who's going to run the corporations when these hippies grow up?" It took no time at all to produce a new generation of what the SDS used to call "bullet-headed make-out artists.") And rock & roll, in a way that is unimaginable now, was the artistic expression of the new society, much as Constructivism was the artistic expression of the new Soviet society. What happened to rock & roll was exactly what happened with Constructivism: it turned into designs for bathroom tiles.

Another thing that weakened the counterculture, at least in the U.S., was that the universities accepted the more superficial demands of the students— among them, that what they study have greater "relevance" to their lives. This meant, for example, in the first stage, that recent books were introduced into literature

135

courses, things people were reading anyway. By the second stage, in the 1980's, this had expanded to recent culture in general— meaning, of course, pop culture— to which the new French theories could be so cleverly applied. So now if you're a student— and nearly all youths are students— and you can study Madonna or *Neuromancer* for a degree, urged on by the professors, the authority figures, well, what then is the counterculture— Sophocles and Milton?

During the pre-Hispanic era, there were people whose function it was to guide others in the taking of drugs, which had a specific meaning. Perhaps what happened in the 60's was the loss of certain norms, certain knowledge under which drugs should be taken.

I think that in the 60's there was a kind of elite who took drugs, until around 1967. At that time, there was a general set of beliefs shared by those who took drugs. An elite, in other words, not of priests, but of believers. By the time of Woodstock, in 1969, the practices, but not the beliefs, had spread to the entire country. For us— white middle-classintellectual New York City kids— Woodstock was not, as it is remembered, the climax of the hippie movement, but a sign that it was over, had gone suburban. The ideology had dropped out, and what was left was a new form of hedonism— one which, however, in retrospect, I wish had lasted: I'll take group mud baths any day over group baptisms.

But nobody I knew went to Woodstock. My friends were far too self-consciously cool to light candles while the dreadful Melanie sang "Beautiful People." That weekend, for example, I was camping on the side of Mt. Shasta, in California, down the stream from a group of people who used to wander naked in the woods, playing flutes. They believed that the mountain was hollow, that it was inhabited by survivors of the lost continent of Lemuria, and that messages from the Lemurians could be decoded from Beatle records.

And yet, from the current perspective, Woodstock belongs to another world: There were no t-shirts sold at Woodstock, no marketing. Ten years later, the symbol of youthful rebellion against bourgeois values would be the most successful business-woman in America: Madonna.

In this century drugs tend to come more from the laboratory than from the natural world. Do you think this has created the absence of sacrality in the consumption of drugs?

Not really. In fact, most drugs require a great deal of preparation. Think of soma, as it is described in the Vedas. It doesn't make a great deal of difference if its origin is the modern laboratory or not: Amazonians preparing ayahuasca are lab technicians in different clothes. But it's true that in the 60's drug-taking was seen as a return to the natural world, a return to the values of the tribe. An attitude that no longer exists, because that was the part of the counterculture that was in opposition to all forms of industrialization— except the manufacture of long-playing records— whereas the hippest kid today is a techno-freak.

It's curious that the counterculture which was opposed to industrialization and capitalism should have created the enor-mous industry of drugs.

That's not entirely true. In the 60's, heroin— the drug of the ghettoes— was controlled by the Mafia, but the hippie trade in marijuana and hallucinogens was carried out entirely by small-scale independent entrepreneurs, the kind of people Mario Vargas Llosa supports these days. It has nothing to do with narcotics traffic as it is now practiced by international cartels.

But this brings up the question of the legalization of drugs. I should say that I am in favor of the complete legalization of all drugs, for all the obvious reasons. Among them, the fact that it would eliminate a huge category of supposed crime — sale and possession, usually of small quantities— with its attendant prison population, now over a million in the U.S., as well as all of the violence associated with drugs: robberies by drug-takers, the wars between the drug-dealers and the police, and the wars among the drug-dealers themselves, with their innocent bystander victims. I can only speak of what has happened in the U.S., but here the vast majority of crimes are drug-related. With legalization this would end overnight. From another angle, I also believe that any activity which involves an individual acting alone, or acting with consenting individuals, without direct effect to others, is not the business of the state, and should not be regulated by the state. This applies to all sorts of activities which have varying degrees of illegality throughout the world: sex of any kind between consenting adults, birth control, abortion, suicide (especially by the terminally ill), and so on.

One often hears the argument against legalization that drugs create anti-social behavior, dangerous to society, and therefore must be prohibited by the state. The newspapers and television are now full of terrifying stories about crack addicts, as they once were about heroin addicts, and before that, so-called marijuana addicts. This is fascinating because crack was called "free-base" when it was used in Hollywood and by Wall Street yuppies, and was not considered to cause psychotic behavior. But when the ghetto discovered the drug, and started using it under a different name, suddenly it became a menace to society. (And in most states, criminal penalties for crack are, not surprisingly, far more severe than those for cocaine.) Similarly, there are many musicians who are life-long heroin addicts, but who have the money to pay for it and lead productive lives, unthreatening to anyone else. And we all know that smoking marijuana did not make us go out and beat up kindly grandmothers, as the propaganda in the 1930's said we would.

There is an interesting parallel phenomenon in the U.S.—besides, of course, the prohibition of alcohol in the 1920's. For most of the century, the state spent a great deal of time and money attempting to eliminate the numbers racket, a form of gambling run by the Mafia. Then in the 1970's the government realized that this could be quite lucrative *for them* and instituted a lottery game that was played in exactly the same way, various combinations of three numbers. That was the end of the criminal aspect of the game: In place of an Evil to be combatted, it was recognized that people will always gamble, that the money could be put to good use, and the police could concern themselves with genuine criminals, murderers and rapists. It happened overnight, and now all the states have lotteries, with the money supposedly going to education.

Drugs, very much like prostitution, should be treated as a health problem, not a criminal problem. Instead of a rhetorical "war" against drugs, there should be a war against what makes people take drugs. Drug use increased enormously in the 1980's because of the economic disaster of the Reagan era. When people have decent lives there is less reason to escape life. This is where the government should be putting its money: legalize drugs and impose a tax on them that would go to improving the infrastructure and treating the addicted.

Anyway, you can't win a war against drugs because it's a war with no end. New soldiers will always appear: it's such an easy way to make money. At the local level, it's the only job in the ghetto that requires no training and guarantees good pay— a salary that is irresistible to many, despite the high risks. At a higher level, drugs are the second biggest industry in the world (after, of course, weapons) and it is well known that they provide an overflowing source of untraceable money for the clandestine activities of many governments. I am not so paranoid as to think that drugs remain illegal in order to serve the interests of the state, but I do think that their illegality is awfully convenient for the state.

What about the relation between drugs and Eastern religions— mystical quests to India, and so on?

Asia has always been the other side of the mirror for the West, so that the leap from the world of hallucinogens to the world of the East is not so great. Moreover in Asia, particularly in India, there is a long tradition of drug use. And India was a place where drugs were easily obtained, and could be taken generally without harassment. To go to India was not only a way to get in touch with the Other, but also a way to find the means for getting in touch with the Other: drugs.

And Mexico, too, of course...

The case of María Sabina, about whom I'd like to write one of these days, is extremely interesting. There was an amazing amount of publicity around her in the 1950's, orchestrated by Gordon Wasson, the banker and mushroom expert who "discovered" her. The world of the "magic mushroom" was a kind of window of subversion in the conformity of Eisenhower America. Suddenly there was this revelation of a world that was entirely different, and it was a tremendous shock. All the major magazines ran articles with titles like "I Ate the Magic Mushrooms," and the Mazatecs were overrun with gringo soul-seekers and Mexican federal police. Sabina claimed that the mushrooms subsequently lost their healing powers, and thus a very ancient practice came to an end, to the delight of the local missionaries from the nefarious Summer Institute of Linguistics, who had brought Wasson there in the first place. But it was much like the enormous publicity around the Beats: Out of nowhere there were these new subversive elements, besides dreaded Communism, that invasion of the body snatchers, in American society.

Like Carlos Castaneda, somewhat later...

Much later— Castaneda's first book is in 1968— after, for example, *Sgt. Pepper*. The difference is that he was a reflection of what was already happening in the U.S. at that time, whereas María Sabina was a contradiction. (That is to say, the image of María Sabina— all this had little to do with the person herself.) She was a radical contradiction of the prevailing values, whereas Castaneda was a confirmation of the new radical values that had been created in part by the discovery of Sabina.

There are other parallels between hallucinogenic experience and poetry, for example the way abstract signs become meaningful, and the experience of synaesthesia: in poetry or under LSD, we hear colors, see smells, touch sounds.

141

One of the great works of synaesthesia is of course Rimbaud's poem where each vowel is associated with a color, and this is absolutely the case with hallucinogens. And this is true in the other arts, for example the pre-Columbian sculpture from Veracruz that we were all looking at the other day in the museum in Jalapa. The ceramic sculptures seem to be emitting sounds because the figures appear to be singing, laughing, screaming— the clay is full of sound. It was extraordinary.

In India the relation between hallucinogens and poetry is explicit. The principal drugs of India today are hashish and bhang, a drink made from hash, but the great drug of classical India, the drug of the Vedas, was soma. Gordon Wasson has persuasively argued that soma was a kind of mushroom, the *amarita muscarina*. And there are some interesting Vedic hymns that deal with how the gods gave soma to humans, and how this coincided with the origin of poetry. In one version, even the various metrical forms of poetry are elaborately tied to the gift of soma. In my own life, I discovered poetry before I discovered drugs. I also discovered that, at least for me, poetry was more profound, more interesting, and more psychedelic than psychedelics. We all have our paths to wisdom, and it merely happened that it was ancient words, not ancient pharmaceuticals, that kept turning me on.

....

IN THE ZÓCALO

[*Written for an issue of Artes de México devoted
to the city of Oaxaca, 1993.*]

Nietzsche, dying, dreamed of moving to Oaxaca to recover his health. Others, myself among them, have dreamed of dying and moving to Oaxaca. For at any moment, and if for only a moment, where I want to be is in its zócalo.

It is more than the touristic pleasure of sitting for hours on the raised platform of the Café El Marquéz, looking out over the cobblestone streets without traffic, the orange blossoms in the canopy of the flame trees, the balloon vendors dwarfed in a kitsch explosion of pink and silver mylar, the kids playing good-natured hide-and-seek with the local halfwit, the strange silence that presses down on the square, even when thousands are viewing the whimsical tableaux of the Night of the Radishes. And it is more than the sensation of being enveloped in the salubrious climate Nietzsche dreamed of— a weather that, here in the north, we receive for one or two days in late spring, and remember the rest of the year. The Oaxaca zócalo is more than the most beautiful Plaza Mayor in Mexico. More than the others, it fulfills the function of all zócalos: a place for doing nothing, sitting at the center of the universe.

A city, traditionally, does not merely contain a sacred or secular center. It *is* a center, surrounded by streets and houses, and from that still center, the "unwobbling pivot" of Confucianism, the power of the city emanates; around it the comings and goings of the world turn. Han Ch'ang-an, two thousand years ago, was the most literal manifestation of this: laid out in the form of the Big and Little Dippers, with the Emperor's Glittering Palace at the place of the unmoving North Star.

In times of insecurity, as in Medieval Europe, the center is found amidst a maze of winding, easily defended streets, all within the confines of defensive moats and walls. In moments of imperial confidence, the city is laid out in a grid, emblem of the new order that has overcome the previous chaos.

Mohenjodaro was the first of the many grid cities, and later, after the luminous Dark Ages, the Italian Renaissance rediscovered it, inspired— it is very Italian— by the chessboard: the little orderly squares as the stage for intrigues, strategies, and assassinations. The Spanish took it from the Italians, and within four years of Columbus' first voyage were erecting their first grid city, Santo Domingo, on the island of Hispaniola. By 1580, there were 273 similar cities throughout New Spain.

[Conquest followed by the replication of monuments to one's self: it is the norm in the West, from the arches of the Romans to the arches of McDonald's. In contrast, consider this bit of Chinese intelligence: when the legendary Founding Emperor Huang-ti defeated a city, he had an exact replica of its palace built in his own capital, to house and retain the vital forces that had once given strength to the fallen city. The Romans, in so many things a conjunction of East and West, gave a proto-capitalist twist to this Asian practice: the *evocatio*, where the local deities of besieged cities were invoked and persuaded to move to Rome, where they would enjoy greater powers.]

Few of the Spanish colonial cities— the great exceptions being México-Tenochtitlán and Cuzco— were built over the pre-Columbian cities: a New World must have its new world order. Oaxaca itself wandered and changed names for a few years: first in 1520 as Villa de Segura de la Frontera near the Zapotec town of Tepeaca; then to the Aztec fort of Huaxyácac; then south to the coast, to the Mixtec kingdom of Tututepec where the climate was too tropical and the natives hostile; and then back again in 1522 to Huaxyácac, as the town of Antequera, and later— it is unclear when— as Oaxaca, the original Náhuatl name having been transformed by Spanish mumbling.

In 1529 the great urban planner of the Empire, Alonso García Bravo, architect of Mexico City and Veracruz, was sent to erect a grid over the razed buildings of the small Aztec fort. The zócalo he laid out, precisely aligned, as centers always are, to the cardinal points, was exactly 100 by 100 *varas* square. To the north, the Aztec direction of death, was to be the cathedral. To the south, municipal buildings. No walls were needed to keep the barbarians out: from the zócalo this balance of sacred and secular power would radiate unobstructed throughout the valley.

To sit in the silence of the zócalo in Oaxaca— a silence that is not from the absence of motion, but rather as though sound had been erased, vacuumed out, from human activity— is to recover that state of perfect rest that can only occur at the center, and that is now so noticeably absent from most of our cities and most of our lives. To dream of sitting in the zócalo in Oaxaca is not to imagine an escape from the world, a shipwreck on a tropical island. It is to imagine an existence— one that can only last a few moments— at the heart of the world: to be completely in the world, but without distraction.

And yet, as always in Mexico, order is always subverted, symmetry is set askew. The central axis at Teotihuacán does not pass through the Temple of Quetzalcóatl; Monte Albán, Mitla, Chichen Itza, and so many others are similarly slightly, intentionally dislocated. Is it an image of the imperfection of the human world, that can imitate, but never rival, heaven? Or is it the emblem of becoming, of forms that are almost, but never quite, fixed? Time, in pre-Columbian Mexico, might have been a nest of perfect circles, one within the other, but the dominant forms were the spiral and the jagged steps. Spiral: from a central point of origin whirling into the unknown. Jagged steps: the least direct way to get from one point to another.

In the zócalo in Oaxaca, one is planted at the center and pulled in two directions. Physically, to the north, to the adjoining little raised plaza beside and the Alameda in front of the cathedral, another hubbub of activity, and a reminder that, slightly off-center, there is always another center. And metaphorically, or historically, to the south, a block from the zócalo, where the municipal market now stands, and where there is the ghost of another center, that of the razed town of Huaxyácac. In its day it too was an ordered and quartered city: six hundred men with their wives and children from each of the principal Aztec provinces, each in its own quarter: Mexicanos, Texcocanos, Tepanecas, Xochimilcas, with other groups scattered on the outskirts.

There are two things to do in the zócalo. First, one must circumambulate, as the new kings of China or Egypt or Cambodia, upon their coronations, were required to circle the sacred center. Circumambulation stakes out one's place in the world; in its democratic form, a territory to inhabit, not to own or rule.

Second, one must sit in that place and let the world continue on. It is an act that is natural in Mexico— as sacred and natural as washing one's hands in India. Yet it is unimaginable in certain other cultures: here, for example, one needs to join an alternative religious group to sit without embarrassment.

Sitting in the zócalo, one's eyes are invariably drawn to the center of the center, to the ornate and Ruritanian bandshell. It is the great late European contribution to this concept of sacred space: that at the absolute center is not a cosmic tree or sacred mountain or pillar of stone— ladders between heaven and earth— but rather an enclosure of empty space. The word *bandshell* captures it perfectly: *band*, the source of music; *shell*, a bounded hollow, a seashell you hold to your ear.

In Oaxaca, the high raised platform of the bandshell is forbidden space, inaccessible to the public— though the children, as if in an ancient parable, always manage to find a way in. Empty by day, packed with local musicians at night. Who cares if the music is less than ethereal? The image that one dreams of is this: at the center of the universe is a perfect and perfectly aligned square; at its center is an empty space; and, at the end of the day, that space is filled with music, a music to reenact the sound that created the universe, the sound that will invent the following day. Time turns, the world turns, around that pivot. Where I'd like to be, right now, is there.

MACDIARMID

[*Written as the introduction to the* Selected Poems of Hugh MacDiarmid, *edited by Alan Riach and Michael Grieve (New Directions), 1993.*]

M y job," he wrote, is "to erupt like a volcano, emitting not only flame, but a lot of rubbish." Heat, fireworks, acrid smoke and tons of dead ash are indeed among his attributes, but a volcano is too small a trope for Hugh MacDiarmid. He occupied— perhaps he was himself— an entire planet.

"Hugh MacDiarmid": the dominant pseudonym among a dozen pseudonyms and one actual birth-name, Christopher Murray Grieve. They wrote about each other, usually in praise, sometimes in disagreement. They were Nietzschean Marxist Christians; supporters of Mussolini and Stalin and Scottish nationalism; followers of Hindu Vedanta. They produced tens of thousands of pages of journalism and commissioned books, edited anthologies and a string of magazines; wrote an autobiography estimated to be 4000 pages long, hundreds of pages of fiction and translations, hundreds of letters to editors and thousands to friends and enemies, and, above all, some 2000 pages of poetry, much of it in long lines. They wrote in variations of two languages, with passages in a few dozen others, even Norn. One of the two primary languages, "synthetic Scots," was their own invention. And behind the curtains of this vast collective enterprise was a short, often miserable and alcoholic man, a nationalist who hated his nation, a gregarious misanthrope who spent most of his life in extreme poverty. All of his teeth were extracted at 24; most of his writing was completed by 50; he died at 86 and never learned to type: MacDiarmid!

The work that will survive begins in 1922, when, at age 30, Christopher Grieve gave birth to Hugh MacDiarmid. At the time he was a nine-to-five journalist for small-town newspapers and a bad Georgian English poet. Most of the passions of his life were already in place: Scottish nationalism, which was flaring all around him, lit by the Irish and Russian revolutions; Marxism; the Social Credit schemes of Major C.H. Douglas, championed by A.R. Orage and Ezra Pound in the *New Age*. His heroes were Nietzsche and Lenin ("I have no use for anything between genius and the working man"), Dostoyevsky for his nationalist spiritualism, and the Russian philosopher Leo Shestov for his evocation of the limitlessness of the imagination, an imagination beyond all dogmas, and where all contradictions are reconciled.

For Scottish writers at the time, the central question was what language to write. Middle Scots, in the 15th and 16th centuries, had been one of the grand vehicles for poetry: the Great Makars Robert Henrysoun and William Dunbar (whom the English call the "Scottish Chaucerians"), Gawin Douglas' magnificent version of the *Aeneid*, Mark Alexander Boyd's single and perfect sonnet, "Venus and Cupid." After 1603— the death of Queen Elizabeth, the transformation of the Scottish James VI into the English James I, and the subsequent loss of Scottish autonomy in the "United Kingdom"— Scots as a literary language decayed. In the 18th century, Allan Ramsay, Robert Fergusson and finally Robert Burns attempted a revival which never quite caught on. (Their greatest contemporary, David Hume, for one, spoke Scots in private but wrote only in English.) Ironically, it was the success of Burns that strangled the movement: Scots became the domain of the corny songs of his imitators, which in turn led to vaudeville parodies. By the time of Grieve's childhood, kids were punished for speaking Scots in school; it was considered unspeakably vulgar.

There was a new Scots Revival movement, led by the various Burns Societies, which Grieve and his pseudonyms had violently opposed as reactionary and irrelevant to the struggle. But by 1922, the wonder year of Modernism, a conjunction of forces changed his mind. His mentor, the militant nationalist Lewis Spence (now remembered as an historian of Atlantis) suddenly switched sides, and supported Scots. There were the examples of the revival of Gaelic in the Irish Republic, and the invention of Nynorsk, a new language created out of various rural dialects, which became the official second language of Norway. There were the writings by Gregory Smith promoting the idea of a unique Scottish psychological make-up: the Caledonian Antisyzygy, capable of holding "without conflict irreconcilable opinions," "easily passing from one mood to the other," and with a "zest for handling a multiple of details"— a perfect description, in fact, of MacDiarmid himself. Moreover, there was the general belief that this sensibility— anticipating, in a way, Benjamin Lee Whorf's studies of the Hopi— could only be expressed by the Scots language. ("Speakin' o' Scotland in English words," MacDiarmid later wrote, was like "Beethoven chirpt by birds.") And most of all, there were the examples of Charles Doughty and James Joyce: Doughty, mining his poems from archaic English, and Joyce, opening the gates for all the world's languages to rush in. From them, Grieve believed that one's spoken language was not enough, that one must ransack the dictionaries for precision of expression.

Grieve created MacDiarmid— and kept MacDiarmid's identity secret for years— as an experiment in writing in Scots. His goal was to return not to the folkish Burns, but to the continental and intellectual Dunbar; to "extend the Vernacular to embrace the whole range of modern culture," as well as to delineate the Scottish mind. By doing so, he thought he would help to sever Scotland from England and insert it into Europe as a nation among equals.

His sources were books like John Jamieson's 1808 *Etymological Dictionary of the Scottish Language* and Sir James Wilson's *Lowland Scotch as Spoken in the Lower Strathearn District of Perthshire*. There he found the words like *watergaw* (an indistinct rainbow) and *yow-trummle* (cold weather in July after sheep-shearing) and *peerieweerie* (dwindled to a thread of sound) that would fill the lyrics of his first important books, *Sangschaw* (1925) and *Penny Wheep* (1926). As one stumbles through these poems now, the eyes bouncing between the lines and the glossary below, it is important to remember that this is exactly how most Scottish readers would have had to read it at the time. (Worse, the glossaries in those early editions were in the back.) MacDiarmid's Scots— and later, much of his English— are written in a language foreign to everyone.

From these early short pieces, which he later dismissed as "chocolate boxes," he set out to write the Scots *Ulysses* or *The Waste Land*, a poem that could demonstrate that Scots was not only a medium for lyrics, but also for the rigorous intellect of difficult "modern" works. The result was *A Drunk Man Looks at the Thistle* (1926), a poem five times as long as Eliot's. Like *The Waste Land*, which makes a cameo appearance in the poem, it is written in a variety of styles and meters— though largely interspersed among ballad stanzas— and it collages other texts: translations of whole poems by Alexander Blok and Else Lasker-Schüler, and some forgotten continentals such as Zinaida Hippius, George Ramaekers and Edmond Rocher, to give the poem a European context. Like "Prufrock" it is an interior monologue, though one that continually locates itself. To *Ulysses'* single day, it takes place in a single night; its Molly is Jean, who similarly has the last word. Its narrative comes from Burns' "Tam o' Shanter" who was also on his way home from the taverns at midnight, and its inspiration from Paul Valery's *La Jeune Parque*, which the French poet described as "the transformation of a consciousness in the course of one night."

A Drunk Man is unquestionably the Scots masterpiece of the century, and nearly all of MacDiarmid's critics and acolytes consider it his greatest work. Certainly it is dense with complexities that are still being unravelled in a parade of monographs, most of them written in Scotland. But it is a curious late Symbolist work in the age of High Modernism. The thistle itself is fraught with significant meaning, and would have appalled the Imagists: emblem of Scotland and the Scottish character, sign of the Drunk-Man's virility, image of the soul flowering over the thorns of the "miseries and grandeurs of human fate"; it even becomes Ygdrasil, the cosmic tree. And its Nietzschean narrative has dated badly: the triumph of the intellect and the soul over drunkenness, psychological difficulties, cultural inferiorities and doubt; the dream of the transformation of the low-born Drunken Man, the poet, into "A greater Christ, a greater Burns"— an odd pair as models for one's superior self. At the end of a century that has seen what can be wrought by acts of "the beautiful violent will," it is MacDiarmid's Nietzschism more than his Stalinism— perhaps they are the same— that is most difficult to take.

Though *A Drunk Man* sold poorly, Hugh MacDiarmid became the most famous poet in Scotland, and Grieve and the pseudonyms shrank in his shadow (except of course when writing articles about him). In the 1920's he edited three magazines, including *The Scottish Chapbook*, which is considered to be the greatest Scottish literary review ever, and contributed to dozens of magazines with "Scots" or "Scottish" in their titles; founded the Scottish chapter of PEN; joined and broke with countless political organizations; stood for Parliament a few times; and held posts in local governments like Convener of Parks and Gardens, Hospitalmaster, member of the Water Board. A hero-worshipper, he read the news from Italy and— as many did at the time— mistook National Socialism for socialism and wrote "A Plea for Scottish Fascism." But his continuing loyalty was to Lenin and Major Douglas and Dostoyevsky ("This Christ o' the neist thoosand years"), believing that the combination of Marxist-Leninism and Social Credit would end the struggle for material existence and prepare the world for the struggle for spiritual transcendence.

In 1933, at age 41, he went into a kind of exile and a prodigious burst of writing perhaps unmatched by any other writer in the century. With his wife, Valda Trevlyn, and son Michael, he moved to a place called Sodom on the tiny island of Whalsay in the Shetlands, paying two shillings a month for a house without electricity and water a quarter of a mile away. The family subsisted on gifts of fish and potatoes from their neighbors and gulls' eggs gathered in the cliffs. In his eight years there, MacDiarmid wrote a series of hack-works, with titles like *Scottish Doctors,*

Scottish Eccentrics, The Islands of Scotland, Scottish Scene; political tracts like *Red Scotland, or What Lenin Has Meant to Scotland* and *Scotland and the Question of a Popular Front Against Fascism and War*; and an autobiography estimated to be a million words long, parts of which were later published as *Lucky Poet* and *The Company I've Kept*. He edited a series of books on Scotland and a large anthology of Scottish poetry, translating the Gaelic sections himself, in collaboration with Sorley Maclean. He was expelled from the National Party of Scotland for Communism and from the Communist Party for nationalism. He had a nervous breakdown and was hospitalized for some months. And there was more:

He set out to write, in English, the longest poem ever written by one individual, *Cornish Heroic Song for Valda Trevlyn*. In the two years between 1937 and 1939, he wrote some six or seven hundred pages of it— one-third of the intended whole. This was virtually all of the poetry (with the exception of *The Battle Continues*), largely unrevised, that he was to publish for the next forty years.

The *Cornish Heroic Song* has never been reconstructed. According to MacDiarmid's biographer, Alan Bold, the first part was a 20,000-line section entitled *Mature Art*. MacDiarmid sent a 10,000-line version to Eliot at Faber's, which the poet admired (while finding the title "forbidding"), but the publisher rejected. Of the surviving longer poems, "In Memoriam James Joyce" (now 150 pages in the so-called *Complete Poems*) was originally merely a piece of *Mature Art*. The "Kind of Poetry I Want" (now fifty pages) was to run throughout the *Cornish Heroic Song*, and "Direadh" (now thirty pages) was to be in a later section. It is unclear where all the other poems belonged, and "Cornish Heroic Song for Valda Trevlyn" itself now survives as an eight-page

154

poem. In 1967 MacDiarmid published a book of poetry called *A Lap of Honour*, containing, he claimed, poems that had been omitted from his 1962 *Collected* because he'd forgotten that he'd written them! Rescued by the scholar Duncan Glen, these contained some of his greatest works, including "Diamond Body" and "Once in a Cornish Garden."

Various forces impel the poems of *Cornish Heroic Song*: First, the attempt to create a "synthetic English," as he had invented a "synthetic Scots," a project inspired by Doughty, but with a vocabulary drawn not, as Doughty had done, from archaicisms, but from the new language of science. It is a poetry of "hard facts," of hundreds of thousands of details ("The universal *is* the particular"), and its ultimate mysticism anticipates the computer age, where an unprecedented precision of measurement and description has only made the universe far more mysterious.

Second, MacDiarmid discovered that the way out of the traditional prosody and rhyme he had hitherto employed almost exclusively was to break prose down into long jagged lines. Often this meant transcribing— the current term is "sampling"— other people's prose: long passages from obscure travel and science books, reviews in *The Times Literary Supplement*, Herman Melville's letters, Martin Buber, Thomas Mann's *Tonio Kröger*. His practice of reproducing these uncredited led to charges of plagiarism later in his life, but plagiarism, to his mind, was besides the point for an epic that was to include everything.

Third, he had come to believe that the poetry of the classless society was not the personal lyric, but an epic without heroes (or with thousands of heroes). And he had taken to heart the words of Lenin's last speech, delivered in 1922 in a prose that sounds like MacDiarmid's, and which are quoted twice in *Lucky Poet*:

It would be a very serious mistake to suppose that one can become a Communist without making one's own the treasures of human knowledge... Communism becomes an empty phrase, a mere façade, and the Communist a mere bluffer, if he has not worked over in his consciousness the whole inheritance of human knowledge— made his own and worked over anew all that was of value in the more than two thousand years [!] of development of human thought.

The result, then, was, in MacDiarmid's words, "an enormous poem," dealing with the interrelated themes of the evolution of world literature and world consciousness, the problems of linguistics, the place and potentialities of the Gaelic genius... the synthesis of East and West and the future of civilization. It is a very learned poem involving a stupendous range of reference, especially to Gaelic, Russian, Italian and Indian literatures, German literature and philosophy, and modern physics and the physiology of the brain, and while mainly in English, utilizes elements of over a score of languages, Oriental and Occidental.

There is nothing like it in modern literature, nothing even close. It is an attempt to return poetry to its original role as repository for all that a culture knows about itself. Unlike Pound's *Cantos*, it does not merely allude to its extraordinary range of referents; it explains everything in a persistent, unorganized stream of erudition to match the Joycean stream of consciousness. Sylvia Townsend Warner described MacDiarmid's autobiography in words that are more applicable to the poetry: "as though the pages of two encyclopedias were being turned by a sixty-mile gale." It is a poetry that wants to raise the standard— both in the sense of hoisting a battle flag and of educating the world through unremitting instruction and admonition— and it is a poetry that, uniquely, keeps reminding us what it ought to be: "The Kind of Poetry I Want."

Certain poems easily detach themselves— among them, the earlier "On a Raised Beach," "In the Slums of Glasgow," "The Glass of Pure Water," "Direadh III," "Diamond Body" and "Once in a Cornish Garden" — and can stand with the poems of the great 20th century poets from the Celtic Isles: Yeats, Basil Bunting, D.H. Lawrence, David Jones. But to excerpt— as editors of various editions of *Selected Poems* have been forced to do— from the poems of *Cornish Heroic Song* is to destroy the effect of MacDiarmid's greatly underestimated music. Based on Scottish piping and Indian ragas, it is dependent on the counterpoint (MacDiarmid would say dialectic) between a continuous drone and bursts of melody. The pleasures of MacDiarmid are precisely the explosions of passion, rage, intellectual insight, aphorism and spiritual transcendence that occur after pages of foreign word-lists and arcane bibliographies, catalogues of scientific terms and theories, histories of literature and art and philosophy and music, piling up, as he wrote, like Zouave acrobats. These are the volcanic fireworks amidst the tons of dead ash; out of context there is no contrast, and their power is diminished. Rather like excerpting the magnificent landscapes from the *Cantos*, they are the jewels without the crown.

He is one the great materialist poets and one of the great mystics; a poet thoroughly immersed in the technicalities of geology, astronomy and physics who could also write "The astronomical universe is *not* all there is" and "everything I write, of course,/ Is an extended metaphor for something I never mention." He was a political animal who believed that the role of the poet is to be a solitary contemplative; a man whose millions of words revolve around a center of absolute stillness: "The word with which silence speaks/ Its own silence without breaking it." A Nietzschean Marxist, he thought that the collective, with all its contradictions, could be embodied by one superior man. A Communist from the working-class (unlike his English poet contemporaries), he had no pity for the poor, but honored them for their stoicism and loathed them for their ignorance and spiritual decay, "innumerable meat without minds." He expressed his love, in "Once in a Cornish Garden," one of the great love poems, through an astonishingly detailed celebration of his wife's clothes and cosmetics. He wrote in a style that owed nothing to the modern writers he most admired: Joyce, Pound, Rilke, Brecht, Mayakovsky, Hikmet. He may be the only poet of the century for whom, in the poem, philosophy matters. Science was his mythology.

He believed that the first civilization was Ur-Gaelic, and that it rose in Georgia, birth-place of Stalin. He started a Hugh MacDiarmid Book Club, which offered subscribers a new MacDiarmid book every two months. He envisioned a Celtic Union of Socialist Soviet Republics (Scotland, Wales, Ireland, Cornwall) which would join in an "East-West Synthesis" with the Soviet Union. He listed his hobby in *Who's Who* as "anglophobia." He believed that Cornwall was an outpost of Atlantis. He rejoined the Party after the invasion of Hungary, while simultaneously signing a public letter denouncing it. He believed that "there lie hidden in language elements that, effectively combined, can utterly change the nature of man." He read his poems under huge portraits of Blake and Whitman in Peking in 1957. He debated on the same side as Malcolm X at the Oxford Union in defense of extremism. He said that "Of all the men I have known, I loved Ezra Pound," but they only briefly corresponded, and had met only once, in 1970, when Pound had already stopped speaking and MacDiarmid was nearly deaf. In his eighties he was writing television reviews. The words he wanted on his tombstone were "A disgrace to the community," but at his death this was ignored.

....

MISLAID IN TRANSLATION

[Written for a talk at Middlebury College, 1993.]

Four years ago, hundreds of thousands demonstrated around the world, thousands rioted, hundreds were wounded and more than a dozen were killed because of a mistake in translation. The mayhem was set in motion by the mere title of what has become the most famous novel ever written, *The Satanic Verses*. As you may know, Salman Rushdie's book was named after a strange legend in Islamic tradition about the composition of the Qu'ran, which was dictated to Muhammad by Allah himself through the angel Gabriel. According to the story, Muhammad, having met considerable resistance to his attempt to eliminate all the local gods of Mecca in favor of the One God, recited some verses which admitted three popular goddesses as symbolic Daughters of Allah. Later he claimed that the verses had been dictated to him by Satan in the voice of Gabriel, and the lines were suppressed. Thus the Qu'ran, as Mircea Eliade has pointed out, is the only divinely revealed text which was subject to revision. (Though God certainly could have used some editorial assistance when he wrote The Book of Mormon.)

What you may not know is that the name "Satanic verses" was an invention of 19th century British Orientalists. In Arabic (and its cognate languages) the verses are called *gharaniq*, "the birds," after the two excised lines about the Meccan goddesses: "These are the exalted birds/ And their intercession is desired indeed." In Arabic (and similarly in other languages) Rushdie's book was called *Al-Ayat ash-Shataniya*, with *shaytan* meaning Satan, and *ayat* meaning specifically the "verses of the Qu'ran." As the phrase "Satanic verses" is completely unknown in the Muslim world, the title, then, in Arabic, implied the ultimate blasphemy: that the entire Qu'ran was composed by Satan. The actual contents of the book were almost irrelevant.

Translators paid for this mistake in translation: On July 3, 1991, the Italian translator of *The Satanic Verses*, Ettore Caprioli, was stabbed in his apartment in Milan. He survived the attack. Days later, the Japanese translator, Hitoshi Igarashi, an Islamic scholar, was stabbed to death in his office at Tsukuba University in Tokyo.

These are, of course, extreme cases— like that of William Tyndale, another sainted translation martyr, strangled and then burnt at the stake in 1535 for the crime of turning the Scriptures into vernacular English— but the point is this: Despite the fact that nearly everything any one of us knows about world literature is due to the work of translators; that nearly every literary renaissance anywhere has been inspired and fueled by translations, the latest news from abroad; despite the fact that people even die for it, translation remains the most anonymous literary profession.

A tiny personal example: Six years ago, I published a 700-page book of the *Collected Poems* of Octavio Paz, at the time the largest volume ever done in English of a 20th century foreign poet. The book— unusually for a book of poetry— was widely reviewed. But consider this: Of about a hundred reviews, eighty-five didn't mention me at all. Ten summed up my work in one word: "excellent," "mediocre," "brilliant," "lackluster." Five gave me a paragraph or two, all of them, even in the rave reviews, complaining about the specific translation of a word or two in some 13,000 lines of complex modern poetry. I use my own case not to elicit pity, but because I happen to have all the clippings: any other translator could tell you the same story. According to reviewers, when we are not invisible, we are merely lively, workmanlike or wooden. And the true measure of our worth— unlike any other writers— is to be found in a few isolated examples of our specific word-choices.

Worse, those of us who translate poetry must suffer the tedious reiteration, in conversation and in print, of that mushy chestnut: Poetry cannot be translated, poetry is that which is lost in translation. To my mind, the untranslatability of poetry is rather like the essential meaninglessness of language or of life: something to ponder for a minute or two, before one gets on with it. As a philosophy, it is not terribly helpful, and, in the case of translation, it manages to wipe out most of world literature for any given individual, and becomes yet another excuse— and one I've actually heard— for not reading.

Of course, for the most doggedly literal, it is true: a slice of German pumpernickel is not a Chinese steam bun which is not a French baguette which is not Wonder Bread. But consider a hypothetical line of German poetry— one I hope will never be written, but probably has been: "Her body (or his body) was like a fresh loaf of pumpernickel." Pumpernickel in the poem is pumpernickel, but it is also more than pumpernickel: it is the image of warmth, nourishment, homeyness. When the cultures are close, it is possible to translate more exactly: say, the German

word *pumpernickel* into the American word *pumpernickel*—
which, despite appearances, are not the same: each carries its
own world of referents. But to translate the line into, say, Chinese, how much would really be lost if it were a steam bun? (I
leave aside sound for the moment.) "His body (her body) like a
fresh steam bun" also has its charm— especially if you like your
lover doughy.

It's true that no translation is identical to the original. But no
reading of a poem is identical to any other, even when read by the
same person. The first encounter with our poetic pumpernickel
might be delightful; at a second reading, even five minutes later,
it could easily seem ridiculous. Or imagine a 14-year-old German
boy reading the line in the springtime of young Aryan love; then
at 50, while serving as the chargé d'affaires in the German con-
sulate in Kuala Lumpur, far from the bakeries of his youth; then
at 80 in a retirement village in the Black Forest, in the nostalgia
for dirndelled maidens. Every reading of every poem is a translation into one's own experience and knowledge— whether it is a
confirmation, a contradiction or an expansion. The poem does
not exist without this act of translation. The poem must move
from reader to reader, reading to reading, to stay alive. The poem
dies when it has no place to go. Poetry is that which is worth
translating.

A few years ago, Bill Moyers did a PBS series on poetry that was
filmed at the Dodge Festival in New Jersey. I had read there with
Paz, and knew that we would be included in the first program.
The morning of the broadcast, I noticed in the index of that day's
New York Times that there was a review of the show. This being
my national television debut, naturally I wondered if their tv critic had discovered any latent star qualities, and I quickly turned to

the page. What he wrote was this: "Octavio Paz was accompanied by his translator,"—no name given of course—"always a problematic necessity."

Down there in Translation Inferno, next to the poetry-can't-be-translated shades are the legions of those who find translation "problematic." These are the people who write nearly all the reviews that mention the translator at all, and they are obsessed, like the Reverend Pat Robertson and Phyllis Schafly, with "fidelity"— in this case, the fidelity to the dictionary meanings of the foreign words. Any lapse in proper behavior— even a one-word stand— is branded a "howler," presumably because they are howling with glee at discovering the transgression. Of course it never occurs to them that the translator, who knows the original better than anyone and has spent months or years on the work, might have *deliberately chosen* to translate the word in a way not immediately apparent to the reviewer's ten seconds of reflection on the matter.

The value of "fidelity" was made clear to me by an interesting experiment I once witnessed: average 9-year-old students at a public school in Rochester, New York, were given a text by Rimbaud and a bilingual dictionary, and asked to translate the poem. Neither they nor their teacher knew a word of French. What they produced were not masterpieces, but they were generally as accurate, and occasionally wittier, than any of the existing scholarly versions. In short, up to a point, anyone can translate anything faithfully.

But the point at which they cannot translate is the point where real translations begin to be made— and it is a point I want to make here. The purpose of a translation into English is not, as it is usually said, to give the foreign poet a voice in English. It is to allow the poem to be *heard* in English. [I use "English" here rather than the usual term in translation-land, "target language"— which seems more appropriate to weapons practice than poetic practice— though of course the translation could be going into any language.]

This does not mean— as many translation enthusiasts and even many translators believe— that the object of a translation is to create an original poem in English. (This is easily refuted by the evidence. The great translations of the century— say, Pound's "Seafarer" or *Confucian Odes*, Blackburn's Provençal or his *Cid*, Rexroth's Li Ch'ing-ch'ao— to name only a few among the dead— would all be ludicrous if they'd been presented as original poems by Americans of the 20th century, even as poems written in the voice of a persona.)

The translation one writes will always be read as a translation. It always, inescapably, carries the geographical and historical context of the original with it. This is not, as it might seem, a burden, but is rather a gift: It gives the translator in English a certain freedom not always available to poets writing in English: the ability to introduce strange elements— musical structures, sounds, phrases, words— that readers will assume are mandated by the original, and possibly accept in ways they wouldn't from a poem in English. (One reason why the partisans of the dullest academic American poetry often turn out to be aficionados of foreign avant-gardes.)

The ideal English translation, then, is one that allows the poem to be heard in English in many of the ways that it is heard in the original. This means that a translation is a whole work— it is not a series of matching *en face* lines— and should never be read as such. It means that the primary task of a translator is not merely to get the dictionary meanings right— which is the easiest part— but rather to invent a new music for the poem in the English, one that is mandated by the original. (Remember Robert Creeley's famous dictum: "Form is an extension of content.") A music that is not a technical replication of the original. (There is nothing worse than translations, for example, that attempt to recreate a foreign meter or rhyme scheme. They're sort of like the way hamburgers look and taste in Bolivia.) A music that is perfectly viable in English, but which— because it is a translation, because it will be read as a translation— is able to evoke another music, even reproduce many of its effects.

This is also why poets are, as is well known, both the best and the worst translators of poetry. They are the best because they are writers and often prodigious readers of contemporary poetry in their own language, at ease with what it sounds like and— more important— with the skill of knowing how far they can go to make it different.

This is why nearly all so-called scholarly translations are so dead on the page: their authors know everything about the foreign language and text, and nothing about how poems are heard in this country at this moment. (Which is also why the opinions of the most strident reviewers of translations— who are usually members of the department of the original's language— are generally suspect. Not to mention their proprietary interests: they have to drum up customers, so naturally they find most translations, except those done by colleagues, to be pale imitations.)

And those poets who have been the worst translators have been precisely those enamored with their own voices, who hear only themselves, are incapable of listening, and therefore of recreating the experience of listening. Translation, at a certain level, is a Zen exercise: it is dependent on the dissolution of the ego.

There is no definitive translation because a translation always appears in the context of its contemporary poetry— and the realm of the possible in any contemporary poetry is in constant flux— often, it should be emphasized, altered by the translations that have entered into it. Any poem should be translated as many times as possible, even by the same translator.

There is no poem that cannot be translated. There are only poems that have not yet found their translators. The translation is never inferior to the original. It is only inferior to other translations, written or not yet written.

Translation is not a means for allowing the foreign to speak. The foreign has already spoken, they don't need us. But we need *them,* if we are not to end up repeating the same things to ourselves. Translation is one of the ways that lets us listen. It expands the range of possibilities of what we, right now, can hear. From listening, we learn to speak. Translation expands what we can write. Which in turn expands what we can hear. Translation is a necessity, not an accessory, one of the pleasures and— despite the titles of every academic conference on the subject— not one of the problems.

....

NOTES FOR *SULFUR* IV

[*Written for the back pages of* Sulfur, 1992-1995.]

East Berlin Poets

Two years ago, *Sulfur* 27 featured a section, edited by Roderick Iverson, on the East Berlin poets in the bohemian Prenzlauer Berg scene. The poet most quoted by Iverson, and the one who opens the section, was Rainer Schedlinski (b. 1956), the editor of a samisdat magazine called *ariadnefabrik*. Iverson speaks of attending an underground reading by Schedlinski and others, and describes the discussions that followed as "being voiced with astonishing moral anger." He cites Schedlinski at length on the poet's need to counter the prevailing enforced silence and self-censorship, and sits with the poet in a former literary hang-out as he laments the defection to the West of many of his friends. Iverson ends the first part of his essay with the collapse of the Wall, and this quote from Schedlinski: "The person who knows how things will proceed from here is a person who is not completely informed..."

That last word has taken on an eerie resonance, for it turns out that throughout the years of the Prenzlauer Berg scene, Schedlinski was a regular, paid informant for the Stasi, the East German secret police. Schedlinski, according to the recently opened Stasi files, sent frequent reports on all his friends: the parties and literary events they attended, the local gossip, off-hand remarks, and so on. At least one poet was, on the basis of this information, arrested.

Schedlinski was hardly alone. Another Stasi employee was Sascha Anderson, a poet and general impresario of the scene— organizer of art shows, rock concerts, magazines, presses, and legendary parties. (Anderson and Schedlinski, though close friends, were probably unaware of each other's secret life.) And from the galactic size of the Stasi files, it is estimated that one out of every fifty East Germans was an informer, including husbands and wives, parents and children reporting on each other. Over 600 friends and acquaintances of the novelist Christa Wolf sent in reports.

There is also the theory, advanced by the poet Wolf Biermann, that the Prenzlauer Berg scene was actively encouraged by the Stasi— that after the highly emotional, political, and accessible poetry of Biermann and his generation (all expelled to the West), the secret police welcomed the endless essays couched in deconstructionist jargon and the kind of poems where, in Schedlinski's words in *Sulfur*, language is "dismantled into the smallest mnemonic unities which [are] mutually purged from the text," or where "one word destroys the one next to it." (Not surprisingly, the Prenzlauer Berg story has curious loops back to the Paul de Man case.)

And another loop: In that same issue of *Sulfur*, responding to my attack on the NEA (as having bought the silence of the artists

169

and writers during the Reagan years), Clayton Eshleman writes: "I've given up on trying to make a connection between source of income and quality of artistic production," that "capable imaginations will do their work" regardless. Many would agree, but it's worth noting that Rainer Schedlinski now claims that the only reason he worked as an informer was to pay for his magazine: "I had no scruples about that. I thought, if the Stasi want to finance the underground— fine."

[Schedlinski and Anderson, meanwhile, have formed a publishing company called Galrev, and Schedlinski has, like most victims and perpetrators these days, made a career of telling his story, in European magazines and on television, and on a lecture tour of the U.S.]

....

Kamau Brathwaite

Nathaniel Mackey's *Hambone* is the main meeting-place for Third World, American minority and white avant-gardists. It is one of the two or three poetry magazines that is always worth reading. The latest issue (#10) features an 80-page poem, "Trench Town Rock," by the Barbadoan poet Kamau Brathwaite, on the violence in Kingston, Jamaica, where he lives. Combining the Dos Passos "camera eye," newspaper clippings, transcripts of radio talk shows, lyric passages, an African folk tale, and a computer-generated typographical montage, it is the kind of knock-down political poem not seen in these parts for twenty years. Visually, he is the first important poet to

explore in depth the possibilities of computer fonts, having created what he calls his "video style."

Brathwaite remains little known in these self-absorbed states.
(In the Caribbean he is something like William Carlos Williams to
Derek Walcott's T.S. Eliot, particularly in his rejection of BBC English as an essential part of working toward a post-colonial
Caribbean identity.) His great works are two trilogies, *The
Arrivants*, from the 1960's, and the unnamed second trilogy from
the 1970's and 1980's, which consists of *Mother Poem, Sun
Poem*, and *X/Self*. Unpublished in the U.S., both trilogies are
compendia of African and Afro-Caribbean history, mythology
and current realities, written in an astonishing array of lyrical and
anti-lyrical forms. Documents, lists, histories, facts, songs, bits of
conversation overheard, sentences copied down: the endless particulars of the world he has collected take him into cosmic celebration, or, its opposite and equal, cosmic rage. He is the great
chronicler and singer of the African diaspora, and one whose formal inventiveness keeps him forever moving. Even more, it is a
glimpse of the territories poetry is just beginning to stake out.

....

Chinese "Obscure" Poets

The Chinese poets of the
"Obscure" or "Misty" group were the aesthetic vanguard of the
student uprisings of the 1970's and 80's— their poems playing a
role quite similar to that of rock music in the U.S. in the 1960's.
Since the Tiananmen Square massacre in 1989, nearly all of these

poets are in exile, and their work is starting to appear in English— though often in translations that require some reader participation in the creation of the text.

Their early work, where they rejected socialist realism in favor of highly subjective lyrics and an independently-invented Imagism, is best represented by the North Point anthology, *A Splintered Mirror*, translated by Donald Finkel and Carolyn Kizer. Since then, each of the poets has been moving in a different direction, and all their books are worth tracking down. Bei Dao's early poems are in *The August Sleepwalker*; the recent work, written in exile in various Northern European countries and full of haunting images that are simultaneously simple and nearly impenetrable, is in *Old Snow* (both New Directions, both translated by Bonnie McDougall). Duo Duo is the most political, surrealist and emotionally charged in the group; his work is in *Looking Out From Death*, translated by Gregory Lee, published in England by Bloomsbury and unavailable here. Gu Cheng has the humor and exuberance of the early European modernists; his "Bulin" poems are eccentric cousins to Rothenberg's Coyote and Cokboy (which he's never read). His *Selected Poems* (various translators) has been published in Hong Kong by Renditions. Yang Lian's major work, a 300-page philosophical poem whose title is an invented character pronounced *I* (as in *I Ching*) has yet to be translated. Meanwhile, two sets of six-line poems are in *Masks & Crocodile* (Canterbury Press, Australia) translated by Mabel Lee with an interesting long introduction.

Since 1989, Bei Dao has been living in Sweden, Denmark, Norway and Germany, and has resurrected his magazine from the 1970's, *Jintian* (Today), for the writers in exile. He is separated from his wife and child, who have not been permitted to leave China. Duo Duo has been living inEngland, Canada and Holland. Gu Cheng, a disciple of Chuang Tzu, has been living on a tiny island off New Zealand, sometimes subsisting on roots and berries. Yang Lian has been in Australia and New Zealand, Berlin and New York. In Aarhus, Denmark, Bei Dao writes that he speaks Chinese to the mirror. Yang Lian writes that the only ones who don't believe words are the poets.

[Postscript, 1995: Bei Dao is now living in the U.S. In 1994 he attempted to enter China to visit his family. He was arrested at the airport, detained and interrogated for a day, and then deported. Perhaps because of the ensuing publicity, in 1995 his wife and daughter were allowed to join him in California.

I met Gu Cheng in 1992 in New York, where he was part of a reading tour of Chinese poets, sponsored by the Academy of American Poets. He was accompanied by his wife, Xie Ye, a poet who has not been translated, and a woman of extraordinary beauty. They were an exceedingly strange couple.

Gu Cheng was clearly modeling himself on one of the Taoist Immortals. He wore a tall cylindrical hat, made from the leg of a pair of blue jeans, in order, he said, to keep his thoughts from escaping. Xie Ye told me that he slept in it. They lived on Wai-heke Island, New Zealand, where they gathered food, and supplemented their income by selling spring rolls in the market. They had a small son with an English name, Samuel, whom they had given, at Gu Cheng's insistence, to be raised by a Samoan family on the island. The boy spoke no Chinese, and Gu Cheng spoke no English.

At dinner, Gu Cheng startled his wife by glancing at the menu and actually selecting a dish. He had never done this before, preferring to merely eat whatever he was given. Our conversation, translated into halting English by Xie Ye, went on for hours. She tape-recorded all of it, because "everything Gu Cheng says should be preserved." She gazed at him raptly throughout; both of them radiated sweetness. But changing the tapes, she told me, smiling, that she hoped Gu Cheng would die, so that she could live with her son again.

His conversation was funny, dizzying, elliptical, ultimately incomprehensible. Any topic quickly turned into speculation on the universe. From the poems he read later that week, it was obvious that Gu Cheng was probably the most radical Chinese poet who ever lived. With little knowledge of Western modernism, he had invented a poetry full of Steinian repetitions, *zaum*-like sounds, eccentric rhythms, and wacky humor. The translations I've seen only hint at this.

On November 11, 1993, on Waiheke Island, Gu Cheng, 37, murdered Xie Ye, 35, with an ax, and then hanged himself. She had told him that she had finally decided to leave.

He had written: "The poet is like the fabled hunter who naps beside a tree, waiting for hares to break their skulls by running headlong into the tree trunk. After waiting for a long time, the poet discovers that he is the hare."]

....

Lorca Collected

For decades García Lorca's heirs deemed all English translations inadequate and refused to grant permission for any new publications. Thus, other than a few samisdat editions like the Blackburn or Spicer, Lorca's poetry languished here for thirty years, represented only by the slim New Directions *Selected* and the monstrous Ben Belitt *Poet in New York*. Finally, in the mid-1980's, as the early work was entering public domain and the family began losing control, the heirs appointed the leading Lorca scholar, Christopher Maurer, as the editor of English-language editions. Maurer assigned *Poet in New York* to two mellow dudes from Oregon who'd never seen the Manhattan skyline, let alone the stoops of Harlem. (OK OK— you don't have to, but it helps. Especially when the tone is metropolitan freak-out.) The result, though infinitely superior to Belitt, was Lorca APRed, laundered and pressed— and, by the way, no better or worse than the five or six manuscripts of the complete text, rejected by the heirs, that I happened to see over the years.

Now Farrar Straus & Giroux has finally published the long-delayed *Collected Poems*, edited by Maurer. At 900 pages, it's a great ball of dough with a diamond inside. A beautiful book, and an authoritative edition of the Spanish texts: virtually the complete poetry (except *Poet in New York*); good intro, excellent notes. But there's gloomy weather on the recto: Maurer has chosen to ignore the many existing published and unpublished translations in favor of entirely new versions. Not necessarily a terrible idea. But he has also, with one exception, equally ignored all the American and English poets— from every possible poetic camp— who occasionally translate Spanish and could have collaborated, and instead given the work to "colleagues" in the Spanish Department, some of them graduate students. What they've produced is hundreds of pages of "Green oh how I love you green" and "No, I refuse to see it!": D.O.A. English that is generally, but not even always, semantically correct.

The one poet in this faculty lounge is Jerome Rothenberg, and his versions of the recently discovered *Suites* is a 250-page section that ejects itself from the rest of the book, and should have been published separately. In Spanish this may not be Lorca at his deepest song, but it is by far the wittiest, most inventive, above all, most musical Lorca in English ever. A tour de force, and a pity we have to pay $50 to hear it.

....

Zukofsky Collected

If you don't have one of the samisdat copies of *80 Flowers*, it has finally been published in available, though expensive, form in the *Complete Short Poetry of Louis Zukofsky* (Johns Hopkins). Otherwise the title is a misnomer and the book a bummer. It essentially reprints the Norton *All*, but does not include the many poems which appeared in magazines and were never reprinted, nor any unpublished material. There are no textual notes. The great Catullus translation is included, but without the Latin facing it, as in the original Cape Goliard/Grossman edition, taking away exactly half the fun of matching the sounds. No editor is listed, for good reason.

The Zukofsky book is further evidence of how badly the American moderns have been neglected by the scholars. (Compare the treatment any Dead French Man gets.) Out past the Litz/Mac-Gowan Williams, the Butterick Olson, the Cooney Reznikoff, the Simon Hart Crane, early Pound, and H.D. (to 1944) the landscape is desolate. It is mind-blowing that there's no complete poetry of Stevens, or Langston Hughes, not even of Frost. Incredible that there's no scholarly edition of Eliot's poetry (the scurrilous poems, for example, have never been published) and that t-here are volumes to be done of his uncollected prose. The Niedecker is a well-known disaster; the Loy, I'm told, is full of mistakes. The *Cantos* keep changing with every reprint. Moore and Oppen, especially, need editions with all the variants (and Oppen a gathering of his extraordinary notes to himself). Other than Pound, there are very few collections of letters. Rexroth and postwar H.D. and Olson's prose and even Robert Lowell need to be put together... The list is endless. Once upon a time the academy used to give us text, not merely its explication.

[*Postscript, 1995:* In 1994, 27 years after his death, *The Collected Poems of Langston Hughes* (Knopf) appeared, edited by Arnold Rampersad and David Roessel. It limits itself to poems previously available in book form, omitting hundreds of unpublished poems and work that only appeared in magazines. Strangely, the political and agit-prop poems of *Good Morning Revolution* (Lawrence Hill), edited by Faith Berry, are also excluded. But it's a chance to read the text of a rare collector's item: *Ask Your Mama* (1961), Hughes'book-length poem, a collage of voices written almost entirely in upper-case letters, and a work similarly ambitious and unrecognized as Duke Ellington's last *Suites*.

In 1995, 32 years after his death, the Library of America announced the publication of a huge *Collected Poems, Prose and Plays* of Robert Frost. Textually, the rest remain a mess.]

....

Poet Laureates

Up there in Prize World, the rule is: when in doubt, tap Mona Van Duyn. She rhymes, she's easy to read, she's cheerful, she's a she, and best of all, a she who writes about how much she loves her hub. Her best-known poem, quoted in every press account every time she wins something, reads in its entirety, as I remember it: "I sometimes think the world's perverse/ But then again it could be worse." The actual humor of this escapes me, but it does retrospectively elevate Ogden Nash to a Karl Kraus-dom of corrosive wit.

Van Duyn has just been crowned our new Poet Laureate, joining the august ranks of Wilbur, Eberhart, Nemerov, Strand and Brodsky. Well so what. But there are a few interesting things about our Laureates. One is that they are all openly heterosexual: certain same-sex epicures in the Establishment have quite obviously been passed over. Two is that, except for Brodsky (a card-carrying anti-communist) they have never, in their careers, expressed any political opinions. (Brodsky, even before he was crowned, used to attend black-tie dinners at the Reagan White House, no doubt fervently discussing Hardy and melancholia over the koho salmon quenelles with Sylvester Stallone and Jerry Falwell.) Three is the real scandal: Throughout the years of the NEA debate and the assaults on art and speech by Senator Helms & ilk, not one of the reigning Poets— Nemerov, Strand, or Brodsky— used his position to publicly rise in defense of literature and free expression. They were all happy campers in the Bush/Quayle administration, abiding by the first principle of their selection: poets who make nothing happen.

[1992]

....

Muriel Rukeyser

In the continuing recovery of neglected American women poets, I'm surprised no one has picked up on Muriel Rukeyser: a strange case of a well-known but unread poet who never really formed alliances with anyone. She started out in the 1930's as a Yale Younger Poet and Communist Party member, but her documentary poetry was too modernist for the Party, too documentary for the modernists, and too modernist and documentary for the ruling New Critics. In the 1940's, although her friendships were with New York literary establishment types, she was notoriously trashed by Randall Jarrell and never fully accepted by them. In the 50's and early 60's she essentially dropped out to raise her child, and had no connection to the clans of the *New American Poets*. In the late 60's she was highly visible as an antiwar activist and wrote some of her best poetry, but— even as late as 1968, was anyone ready for a long lyric poem that begins with the lines: "Whoever despises the clitoris despises the penis/Who ever despises the penis despises the cunt"?

In 1979, a year before her death, Norton published a massive *Collected Poems*, full of wonderful and awful poems, and strange items like a book-length poem on the life of Wendell Wilkie. All her work was out of print in the 80's. Now Triquarterly has published a selected poems edited by Kate Daniels, appropriately called *Out of Silence*. It's not bad, but the more conventional work is emphasized, and the book itself disfigured by the reiteration of the least appropriate dingbat in memory— an uncoiled tasselled curtain tie between every poem. Norton is planning a *Reader* of her poetry and prose, and a biography by Daniels is in the works. Meanwhile, *Out of Silence* is a place to begin, but it's far more interesting to dig up a copy of the *Collected* and wander by one's self.

....

Myung Mi Kim

Best first book I've read recently is Myung Mi Kim's *Under Flag* (Kelsey St. Press). Kim, born 1957, is a Korean-American woman who came to the U.S. as a child. Hers is a "poem with history," and her history is the Korean War and the American occupation under the flag of which she was raised. Further evidence that the entry of history into the poetry written by American women is an engaging, sometimes thrilling, recent development. A way pointed to by Rukeyser and Lorine Niedecker (however obscured by Niedecker's male handlers: look at what Corman left out of the *Selected*)—but the major influence here is, of course, Susan Howe. History as her story not only opens an infinite possibil-

180

ity of subject matter, but also strange and fresh takes on the language used to tell the tale of the tribe. Only white boys think content is dead.

....

Blaise Cendrars

Blaise Cendrars is the great comet of French poetry. Born in 1887 in Switzerland, his life would take pages to summarize: perpetual traveller from Vladivostok to Rio to Hollywood, poet, filmmaker, merchant seaman, soldier who lost an arm in World War I, publisher, journalist, novelist, resistance fighter in World War II— a man actively involved with nearly everyone, in all the arts, in the Modernist explosion. Though he lived until 1961, all of his poetry was written in the twelve years between 1912 and 1924. (After that, he wrote prose.) Among those works is the single greatest poem-object of the century, the 1913 *Prose of the Trans-Siberian* published as a folding seven-foot sheet covered with hallucinatory colors by Sonia Delaunay. For some reason, he has been less known in the US than his contemporary and equal, Apollinaire. The best previous edition, the New Directions *Selected Writings*, with lively translations by John Dos Passos, among others, is long out of print. But now we have Ron Padgett's translation— an instant classic— of Cendrar's *Complete Poems* (University of California Press), and the Cendrars' comet, on a 76-year cycle like Halley's, is once again visible over North America.

These funny, reportorial, documentary, sentimental, sometimes found poems were ultimately a dead end. (Perhaps because they had no imitators, they remain lively and— except for the occasional whore-with-heart-of-gold— undated.) After Baudelaire and Rimbaud, French poetry splits: One road whose first prominent landmarks are Mallarmé and Valéry and Reverdy and which runs to the present; the other which begins and ends with Cendrars and Apollinaire. Though there's an argument to be made that "Zone" is the most internationally influential poem of the century, one can only imagine a French poetry that would have followed Apollinaire and Cendrars: physical rather than metaphysical, funky rather than serene, full of slang. A poetry that could have recognized— might even have translated!— Pound and Williams. And, as the world followed France for most of the century, changed the poetry everywhere else.

....

Will Alexander

Whenever I hear or read the professors (or worse, the poet-professors) talking about "marginalization" (or worse, their own marginalization) I think of Will Alexander. In a country where poets are hidden from society but known to each other, Alexander writes on, almost totally hidden from other poets.

He was born in 1948 and has spent his entire life in Los Angeles. In twenty-odd years of prolific writing, he has only published

182

one small pamphlet of prose poetry (*Vertical Rainbow Climber*, Jazz Press, 1987) and has appeared in exactly eight magazines. He lives entirely outside of the pobiz world of prizes, grants, readings, teaching positions— at the moment, he is working in the tickets department of the Los Angeles Lakers basketball team. In his latest project, he is two-thirds through a trilogy of novels, *Sunrise in Armageddon* (*Pandora's Hatchery* and *Isolation, Neutrality, and Limbo* are completed) which are paralleled by a trilogy of collections of poems (so far, *Impulse & Nothingness* and *The Stratospheric Canticles*).

His work resembles no one's, and is instantly recognizable. In part, he is an ecstatic surrealist on imaginal hyperdrive. He is probably the only African-American poet to take Aimé Césaire as a spiritual father (and behind Césaire, Artaud and Lautréamont). But he is also, like Hugh MacDiarmid— a writer of utterly different temperament— a poet whose ecstasy derives from the scientific description of the stuff and the workings of the world. His erudition and vocabulary, like MacDiarmid's, are vast: read Alexander with a dictionary and you'll see how precise he is.

No subject seems alien to him: Who else would write a long poem on the death of the Albanian dictator, Enver Hoxha? Who else would attempt to inhabit the brain of an animal in ecological catastrophe? Who else could spin a 40-page poem ("The Stratospheric Canticles") from the verb "to paint"? — a poem that not only ranges through the history of world art, but which is an extended meditation on the way seeing is transformed, by the chemical compounds of paint, into vision.

Will Alexander, one of my favorite writers, is a poet who lives by the old injunction, "Astonish me!"

[1993]

An Anthology of Anthologies

The *Columbia Anthology of American Poetry*, edited by Jay Parini, 750 pages from Anne Bradstreet to Louise Glück, is being heavily promoted as the new standard; it's even a Book-of-the-Month selection. For *Sulfur* readers, it will only be of sociological interest for those who are amused watching the glass-enclosed elevators of literary reputation. Thus, Zukofsky, Reznikoff, Olson, Creeley, and Duncan have now been admitted, but they are grudgingly allotted one or two pages each. Oppen, Rexroth, Spicer, Blackburn, Everson (among the dead) are still nobody. Of *Sulfur* contributors, only Ashbery, Snyder, Ginsberg, and Baraka are included. The major living poets are, according to the page-count, Levine, Ashbery, Pinsky, Rich, and Gwendolyn Brooks. Fame in America, as ever, is once again proved fleeting: prize-winning poets of yesterday and today such as the Benets, van Doren, Gregory, Zaturenska, Karl Shapiro, X.J. Kennedy, Kizer, Kumin, Logan, Simpson, Dugan, Bly, Meredith, Swenson, Hugo, Howard are history, and Merwin (called "William S." as he was in the 1950's) gets slapped in the face with a single page, no better than some avant-gardist. Meanwhile Teasdale, Wylie and Winters linger on, and a host of future unknowns are introduced.

In the new Multi-Culti world, there are many more women and African-Americans then there used to be in such books— particularly a lot of (usually justifiably) forgotten women from the 19th century— but the redressing of imbalance does not extend to Loy, Stein or Niedecker. Among the women, there is one scandal and two surprises: Dickinson still remains too radical for these oak-panelled walls: though praised in the introduction, she's given less space than Longfellow and, almost unbelievably, her punctuation has been "normalized" (as they used to call it)—even now, after forty years of the Johnson edition and a thousand monographs on her dashes. (Would a *Columbia History of Art* put black bars across the nudes?) Moore and Millay are definitely in the UP elevator: Moore, in number of pages, is the third greatest poet of the century, after Eliot and Stevens (followed by Frost, Lowell, Merrill and Pound); and Millay gets the same space as Williams.

The brief introduction is most notable for this piece of Newt jingoism: "The modernist movement in poetry was largely American in its origins." We also learn that Imagism was "founded by Amy Lowell and H.D. and joined by Ezra Pound," and has been an important influence on the (otherwise unmentioned) "language" poets, and that *The Cantos* "has failed to convince anyone but a few isolated critics of its greatness." The book, unusually for a university press publication, contains no bibliography or any notes on the individual poets.

But there's more: I became interested in the book after a glance at the table of contents. Charles Olson was represented by one short poem,"Poem 143: The Festival Aspect." This happens to be a poem I included as part of the Olson section in my anthology, *American Poetry Since 1950: Innovators & Outsiders*. Buried in the third volume of *Maximus*, it is little-known: not included in the Olson *Selected Poems*, or reprinted elsewhere. There was no way in hell, in thicket, that another anthologist— particularly one with no apparent interest in Olson— would have independently selected the same short poem from Olson's vast work. Clearly Parini had read my book.

I started checking out the other poets whom we both include, and found various cases where Parini repeated part of my selection for an individual poet. Some of these were not terribly unusual: poems by Baraka, O'Hara and Zukofsky that are not often anthologized, but are not especially obscure. The give-away was a poem by Rukeyser, "Iris": I had pulled it out of her huge *Collected*, both as a poem I liked and to bounce off a poem by Sobin called "Irises." Rukeyser's "Iris" has never been reprinted in an anthology, and isn't even included in either the Rukeyser *Reader* or *Selected Poems*. The other poem in Parini's Rukeyser section was "Then I Saw What the Calling Was," also an unusual choice. I had a hunch Parini hadn't discovered it in the poet's own books. When I tracked it down— in Fleur Adcock's *The Faber Book of 20th Century Women's Verse*— I also found Parini's complete selection for Josephine Miles.

Small wonder I began to wonder what other anthologies Parini had been reading, and, limiting myself to the 20th century poets from James Weldon Johnson to Louise Glück— assuming their "canon" to be less petrifiedthan the 19th— I compared selections. It turned out that, with merely a cursory search through a handful of other books, I could account for two-thirds of the poems and almost two-thirds of the complete or nearly complete sections for individual poets. One-third of the poems was taken from Richard Ellman's *The New Oxford Book of American Verse*. If we add Ellman and Robert O'Clair's *The Norton Anthology of Modern Poetry* we have nearly half the poems. Even more blatantly, in a book that pretends to be a new multicultural reading, all of the Native American poems came from one anthology, Duane Niatum's *Carriers of the Dream Wheel*, and all of the poems for six African-American poets (and most of a seventh) are from the old 1938 James Weldon Johnson *Book of American Negro Poetry*.

These anthologies were apparently supplemented, to a lesser degree, with poems from J.D. McClatchy's *The Vintage Book of Contemporary American Poetry*; Stuart Freibert & David Young's *Longman Anthology of Contemporary American Poetry*; and Robert di Yanni's *Modern American Poets: Their Voices and Visions*.

Here's the breakdown:

SELECTIONS ENTIRELY OR LARGELY DRAWN FROM OXFORD: Vachel Lindsay; Robinson Jeffers; T.S. Eliot; Archibald MacLeish; e.e. cummings; Hart Crane; Allen Tate; Delmore Schwartz; Robert Duncan; Denise Levertov; A.R. Ammons; Sylvia Plath; Carl Sandburg (3/6); H.D. (4/6); Conrad Aiken (2/3); Elizabeth Bishop (4/7); James Merrill (3/6).

SELECTIONS ENTIRELY OR LARGELY DRAWN FROM MCCLATCHY: W.D. Snodgrass; Galway Kinnell; Anne Sexton; Robert Hass; Randall Jarrell (2/3).

SELECTIONS ENTIRELY DRAWN FROM WEINBERGER: Louis Zukofsky; Charles Olson.

SELECTIONS ENTIRELY DRAWN FROM JOHNSON (AFRICAN-AMERICANS): James Weldon Johnson; Paul Laurence Dunbar; Claude McKay; Gwendolyn Bennett; Arna Bontemps; Countee Cullen.

SELECTIONS ENTIRELY DRAWN FROM NIATUM (NATIVE AMERICANS): N. Scott Momaday; Simon J. Ortiz.

SELECTIONS ENTIRELY DRAWN FROM NORTON: Jean Toomer; Marilyn Hacker.

SELECTION ENTIRELY DRAWN FROM ADCOCK: Josephine Miles.

SELECTIONS ENTIRELY OR LARGELY DRAWN FROM LONGMAN: Donald Justice; Nancy Willard; Charles Wright (4/6).

SELECTIONS ENTIRELY DRAWN FROM DI YANNI: Robert Creeley; James Tate.

SELECTIONS ENTIRELY OR LARGELY DRAWN FROM COMBINATIONS OF THESE ANTHOLOGIES:

Oxford plus *Norton*: John Crowe Ransom.

Johnson plus *Norton*: Langston Hughes.

McClatchy plus *Norton*: Richard Wilbur; Gary Snyder; Theodore Roethke (5/8).

Weinberger plus *Norton*: Frank O'Hara; Allen Ginsberg; Amiri Baraka.

Longman plus *Norton*: William Stafford.

Longman plus McClatchy: Robert Hayden.

Adcock plus Weinberger: Muriel Rukeyser.

Oxford plus McClatchy: John Berryman (5/6); Robert Lowell (6/7); James Wright (4/5).

Oxford plus di Yanni: Robert Frost; Ezra Pound; Marianne Moore.

Oxford plus di Yanni plus *Longman*: Wallace Stevens (9/10).

These are the sources I could track down in an afternoon; it is probable that a more diligent researcher could find more. [The poets I couldn't find generally fall into two groups: women from earlier in the century— Amy Lowell, Teasdale, Wylie, Millay, Adams, Riding— which possibly indicates an anthology I missed, and contemporary poets, many of them Parini's colleagues at Bread Loaf, whom it must be assumed that he actually reads.] To the inevitable response that many poems are "canonical" or "anthology pieces," it's worth noting that for certain poets— among them, Stickney, Williams, Penn Warren, Brooks and Rich— Parini has clearly made his own choices. And it's interesting to compare Helen Vendler's *Harvard Anthology of Contemporary American Poetry* or Hayden Carruth's *The Voice That Is Great Within Us*, which, covering many of the same poets, rarely overlap with Parini. McClatchy and Ellman are quite different, and even Ellman (the secret and unwitting co-editor of this book) going from the *Oxford* to the *Norton*, only repeats himself half the time. Love them or hate them, it is obvious that Vendler, Carruth, McClatchy, and Ellman— or, more recently, Paul Hoover and Douglas Messerli— have done what an editor of an anthology is supposed to do: offer a reading pitched between history ("canon") and an evident personal taste, based on a fairly thorough knowledge of the individual poets. With the exception of a few poets whom Parini obviously has read in depth, his book is, far beyond coincidence, a half-hearted recapitulation of a few other anthologies. This may not, strictly, be plagiarism, but it's as close as an editor can get.

[1995]

....

PAZ IN INDIA

[*The fourth part of the essay "Paz in Asia" originally written for the*
catalog Octavio Paz: Los privilegios de la vista *(Centro Cultural/*
Arte Contemporáneo, Mexico, 1990) *and reprinted in* Outside Stories.
Revised and expanded for the book Archivo Blanco, *edited by*
Enrico Mario Santí *(Ediciones del Equilibrista, Mexico), 1994.*]

T he god Vishnu appears at the
cave of an ascetic, Narada, who has been practicing austerities
for decades. Narada asks the god to teach him about the power
of *maya*, illusion. The god beckons Narada to follow him. They
find themselves in the middle of a burning desert. Vishnu tells
Narada he is thirsty, and asks him to fetch some water from a village he will find on the other side of the hill. Narada runs to the
village and knocks at the first door, which is opened by a beautiful young woman. He stares at her and forgets why he has come.
He enters the house; her parents treat him with respect; the following year they are married. He lives in the joys of marriage and
the hardships of village life. Twelve years go by: they have three
children; his father-in-law has died and Narada has inherited the
small farm. That year, a particularly fierce monsoon brings
floods: the cattle are drowned, their house collapses. Carrying his

children, they struggle through the water. The smallest child slips away. He puts the two children down to search for her; it is too late. As he returns he sees the other two children swept off; his wife, swimming after them, is pulled under. A branch strikes Narada on the head; he is knocked unconscious and carried along. When he awakes he finds himself on a rock, sobbing. Suddenly he hears a voice: "My child! Where's that water you were bringing me? I've been waiting nearly half an hour." Narada opens his eyes and finds himself alone with Vishnu on the burning desert plain.

Maya: it is the "plot" of the first two sections of *East Slope* (Ladera este). The book opens with the lines "Stillness/ in the middle of the night"*— the poet is alone on a balcony overlooking Old Delhi— and then it immediately fills, overflows, with Indian stuff: monuments, landscapes, a jungle of specific flora and fauna, painters, musicians, gardens, gods, palaces, tombs, philosophy, temples, history, bits of Indian English, a large cast of strange and funny characters— the only characters in Paz's poetry— and, central to it all, the lover/ wife. In the end, in "A Tale of Two Gardens" (Cuento de dos jardines)," it all vanishes: "The garden sinks./ Now it is a name with no substance.// The signs are erased:/ I watch clarity."** The poet is not in the desert, but in the middle of the equally empty ocean on a boat leaving India. (Although— this being poetry and not philosophy— his wife, rather than Vishnu, is with him.)

*Quieta/en mitad de la noche.

**El jardín se abisma./Ya es un nombre sin substancia.// Los signos se borran:/ yo miro la claridad.

191

Maya is made manifest by time. The Indian cosmos is a map of ever-widening concentric cycles of enormous time: millions of human years with their perpetual reincarnations are merely one day and night in the millions of years in the life of Brahma, who is himself but one incarnation in an endless succession of Brahmas. The function of yoga and other meditation practices is to break out of these cycles of illusory births and rebirths, off the map (out of the calendar) and into the undifferentiated bliss of *nirvana* (which the Buddhists would later say was equally illusory).

Myth is a similar rupture of time. Its time is intemporal time, and though its narration unfolds in measured minutes and hours it abolishes time with its narration. Narrator and auditor are projected into a sacred space from which they view historical time and all its products: a world to which they must return, but to which they return educated.

The poem too, though heard in a time that has its own precise measurements (prosody), erases time by projecting us into a world where everything looks the same but is more vivid, where we speak the language but it doesn't sound like the language we speak, where ideas and emotions become concrete particulars, and the concrete is a manifestation of the divine.

The first two sections ("East Slope" and "Toward the Beginning") of *East Slope* are "travel poetry": a poetry of verifiable landscapes, things and people which are foreign to the author. But they are among the few instances in the last two hundred years of a travel poetry worth reading. (Poets, since the birth of Romanticism, have tended to write their travels in prose and letters.) One reason is its precision of observation, its glittering language, intellectual cadenzas, emotional and erotic rhapsodies. But more: on nearly every page are synonyms of silence and stillness. The poems are simultaneously located in India and in a not-India, a somewhere else.

As Aztec shamans would travel out of the earth to a place where all time was visible in a state of total immobility. There they could observe the life-force of the *tonalli* at any given moment before it occurred in human life. The shaman's task was to alter the *tonalli*, to effectively rewrite the future.

As the first two sections of *East Slope* observe the world from a world where the wind comes simultaneously from everywhere, where "the present is perpetual" and bodies "weigh no more than dawn."

Paz, above all, is a religious poet whose religion is poetry. This does not mean that the poet is a "little God," as Huidobro dreamed, with extraordinary powers. Rather it is the poem that opens a hair-line crack in time through which the poet, in astonishment, slips through.

The final third of *East Slope*— the long poem "Blanco"— is both the most "Indian" poem in the book, and the one with the fewest images of India. In fact, only three words in the poem pertain specifically to India: the *neem* tree and the musical instruments *sitar* and *tabla*. Only three more refer to phenomena that exist in India and other places, but are not universal: *crow, jasmine, vulture*. Certain words from Indian iconography which one would expect in the text are noticeably absent: *lotus, diamond, skull, moon, wheel*. And four place-specific words signal its universality: *Grail, Livingstone, Castille, Mexico.*

The form of the poem, originally published on a single vertical folded sheet in black and red type—"black and red ink" in Nahu-atl means "wisdom"— is usually described as descending from Mallarmé's *Un Coup de Des...*, as well as the Indo-Tibetan man-dalas and Indian tantric scrolls indicated in Paz's notes. Mallar-mé's poem, however, although it plays with varying typefaces and blank space, still uses a traditional (though oversize) page as its playing-field: it exists to end up in a book. It is more likely that the Western grandparent of "Blanco" is the original 1913 edi-tion, designed by Sonia Delaunay, of Cendrar's "Prose of the Transsiberian." It too is a floor-to-ceiling vertical sheet with dif-ferent typefaces in black and red, but unlike "Blanco" the words are not surrounded by emptiness: every inch is covered with Delaunay's hallucinogenic color, itself a kind of Indian festival.

On the Eastern side, the poem was clearly originally conceived as a simplified mandala. Mandalas have been called "psychocosmo-grams": maps of the universe that are maps of the self. They are simple or complex configurations of nesting circles and squares, drawn on paper or painted oncloth for personal meditation, or laid out with colored powders on the ground for ritual practices. The earliest mandalas were simple geometric figures, sometimes containing letters or words. The later, Tibetan versions are riots of activity, filled with often terrifying iconic images of the gods. They are based on extremely complicated sets of four, which are endlessly elaborated in the esoteric texts for the initiates, called Tantras: four directions, four colors, four goddesses, four joys, four defects, four moments, four gestures, four requisites, and so on— always with a fifth at the center. The construction of a man-dala, and the meditation on it, begins at secular nothing, and pro-ceeds from the creation of *samsara* (all the things of the world), to the reconciliation of all opposites, to, finally, the enlightenment of *nirvana*, sacred nothing. In the words of Giuseppe Tucci, whose *The Theory and Practice of the Mandala* was one of the books that informed the writing of "Blanco," it is a "scheme of disintegration from the One to the many and of reintegration from the many to the One, to that Absolute Consciousness, entire and luminous, which Yoga causes to shine once more in the depths of our being." The Four Moments in the creation of a mandala could equally refer to the progression of "Blanco": they are, in order, Variety, Development, Consummation, Blank.

"Blanco" was apparently modeled as a simplified version of the mandala described in great iconographic detail in an Indo-Tibetan text, composed in 690, called the *Hevajra Tantra*, a line of which Paz uses as an epigraph. The poem, of course, has no gods, other than poetry, and its representational imagery tends to be abstract. But it largely follows the general outline for the *Hevajra Tantra* mandala, which is conceived as a *stupa* seen from above, with a center dome, four walls, four doors with two columns at each door, and four portals. [The *stupa*, like a pyra-mid, is a representation of the cosmic mountain, and— unlike the cave, the cathedral, or the consecrated ground— it is the only sacred space that cannot be entered or climbed. It can only be cir-cumnavigated— much as this essay, or perhaps any reader, does around "Blanco."]

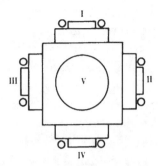

According to this schema, V. represents the center column sections at the beginning and end of the poem, and I.-IV. the four sections consisting of acenter column and one left and right column each. As explained in Paz's notes, I. (North) corresponds to yellow, fire, and sensation; II. (East) to red, water, and perception; III. (West) to green, earth, and imagination; IV. (South) to blue, air, and understanding. V., presumably, corresponds to white, the color of the Absolute. [This slightly rearranges the traditional Indian color-direction correspondences, which are: N: yellow; E: red; W: white; S: blue; Center: green. Curiously, the Aztec correspondences were nearly identical: N: black; E: red; W: white; S: blue; Center: green.]

Although not indicated by Paz's notes, it is also apparent that the poem follows what the *Hevajra Tantra* calls the Four Joys:

I. corresponds to what is called the First Joy. It is devoted to the consecration of the body (here a baptism of fire); its name is The Jar ("vase," "chalice," and "Grail" in the poem), and its accompanying gesture— there are, of course, Four Gestures— is the smile ("you laugh— naked"). The creation of a mandala always begins with the placing of a jar— symbol of the initiate's body—

into which the gods are to descend. It is interesting that into this jar Paz has placed a sunflower, perhaps William Blake's, which was, like a Hindu or Buddhist adept before Enlightenment, "weary of time."

II. is Perfect Joy, known as The Secret. It is a washing away of speech (as throughout this section), and its gesture is the gaze ("I watch myself in what I watch,"*etc.).

III. is Joy of Cessation, known as Knowledge of *Prajna*, with *prajna* in the Tantric texts meaning both "wisdom" and "a woman's body" ("naked place/ in a naked woman"**," etc.). It is a washing away of impurities of the mind, and it is also associated with thunder— as the storm in the central column suggests. Its gesture is the embrace, and it is at this point that the two columns come together.

IV. is Joy Innate, called the Fourth Consecration. Here body, mind and speech are all consecrated, as throughout this section, and its gesture is union, as in the sexual intercourse which becomes explicit in this part of the poem.

The problem of modeling a poem on a mandala, although both unfold in time, is that a poem tends to proceed vertically, while a mandala moves in four directions simultaneously. For this reason, "Blanco" also takes some of its formal arrangement from the yogic and tantric vertical scrolls which depict the ascent of the *kundalini* (the "serpent power" of latent energy). Such scrolls represent the human body, though an outline of the body itself is rarely shown. From bottom to top are images of the seven *chakras*, the energy centers that run from the base of the spine to the

Me miro en lo que miro.

**Paraje desnuda/en la mujer desnuda.*

197

top of the head, and through which the *kundalini* ascends during yogic meditation or tantric practice. Each of the *chakras*, almost needless to say, has a host of attributes: elements, colors, senses, planets, emotions, philosophical concepts,and so on. As an early Hindu commentator wrote, "there are no places of pilgrimage like those within one's own body."

"Blanco," which must necessarily be read down the page (it not being written in Maya) can be seen, loosely, as an upside-down diagram of the *chakras*. Its first two vertical sections (before it splits into left and right) correspond to the first *chakra* at the base of the spine, *Muladhara*, which means "the foundation" (the first two lines of the poem are: "*el comienzo/ el cimiento*" or "the beginning/ the foundation") and which is associated with the *bija*, the syllable-seed (the next two lines are: "*la simiente/ latente*" or "the seed/ latent") which is also the dot that is the literal starting-point for the mandala. The *bija* is the sound of potentiality, and represents pure thought. It is created by the union of *ali* (vowel) and *kali* (consonant), and from it all sound, all language, and everything in the cosmos is born. Other attributes of the *Muladhara chakra* are the earth ("escalera de escapulario"— an earth-body pun meaning both "mineshaft/scapulary ladder"— in what is otherwise meant to be the "fire" section) and the previously mentioned color yellow ("yellow//chalice of consonants and vowels")*.

From there the *kundalini* rises as the poem descends through the other *chakras*— though not strictly: most of the attributes of the

---

Amarillo/caliz de consonantes y vocales.

chakras are present in "Blanco," though not quite in the same order. It never reaches the final, seventh *chakra*, the "illumination of the void": to do so, in a poem,would be less presumptuous than impossible: at that point poetry ceases to be written. (As the *Hevajra Tantra* says, "Nothing is mentally produced in the highest bliss, and no one produces it.") But it does, following this schema, reach the sixth, called *Ajna* ("power"). That is the point between the eyebrows (the last word of the poem is *mirada*, "gaze"), where all the elements return in purified form (as they do in the poem), and whose "color" is transparency ("Transparency is all that remains."*) Its reigning god is Ardhanarishvara, who is the half-male, half-female incarnation of Shiva, the union of all opposites ("No and yes" and the many other pairs which unite in this section of the poem). And it is associated with *nada*, cosmic sound, which becomes a complex Spanish-Sanskrit pun in "Blanco": "*son palabras/ aire son nada*" (with *son* meaning both "sound" and "they are," and *nada* both "nothing" and "cosmic sound"): "sound (they are) words/ air sound (they are) nothing (cosmic sound)." The seed-syllables, though made of air, form words, form the cosmic sound, form the universe. The three are inextricable, and equally illusory: Sanskrit *nada* is Spanish *nada*. [There is a form of meditation, rather like "Blanco," called *nada-yoga*, which consists of focusing on a succession of sounds as they emerge from and retreat into silence.]

Further, in this map of the Hindu body and of "Blanco," there are three "nerves" or "veins" which convey sacred breath and the body's subtle energies. The left, *lalana*, is feminine and associat-

La transparencia es todo lo que queda.

ed with the moon, wisdom, emptiness, nature, the Ganges river, vowels. The right, *rasana*, is masculineand associated with the sun, intellect, compassion, method, the Yamuna (the other great river in India), consonants. In the center is *avadhuti*, the union of the two veins and all their attributes. Again, a schema followed loosely in the poem through its left, right and center columns.

The map of the body is a map of the earth is a map of the cosmos (or time) is a map of language. Most of Paz's work is, and has always been, concerned with the tangle of correspondences among these four elements, their identicalness, their transformations into one another. He is surely Western poetry's primary "inventor of India for our time" (as Eliot called Pound the inventor of China); but he is equally an invention of India: "Indian" readings are possible for poems he wrote long before he went there.

Much has been written about the connections between "Blanco" and the ritual copulation practiced in Tantrism: an escape from the world (and a return to the original unity of the world) through the union of all opposites as incarnated in the actual bodies of the male and female adepts. (The best texts on this are still Paz's pages in *Conjunctions and Disjunctions* and the essay "Blank Thought" in *Convergences*.)

Robert Duncan, in the era of "action painting" in the 1950's, used to emphasize that the poem "is not the record of the event, but the event itself." "Blanco," though far too structured to be an "event" of writing in the processual sense developed by the Black Mountain poets, demands reader participation in the creation of the text by offering a list of variant readings that is, moreover, deliberately left incomplete. Writer and reader are yet another pair of opposites who unite in the poem.

But "Blanco" goes even further: with its male center column and female split columns, it is, uniquely in erotic poetry, a poem that makes love to itself. (As, in India, the syllable-seeds engender language without human assistance.) The author has closed the door behind him on his way out; like Duchamp's *Etant donnés*, it remains for the reader to peer (or not) through the keyhole.

Tantric texts are written in *sandha*, which Mircea Eliade translates as "intentional" language. Each word carries a long string of associative possibilities, like those attributed to the three yogic "veins" above: the spiritual words have materialist and erotic meanings, and vice-versa. (The "right-hand" group of Tantrists believes that all of the material words should be taken only as metaphors for the spiritual; the "left-hand" group believes that all of the spiritual words are merely code names for aspects of the rituals, which, like copulation on a cremation ground, are scandalous to outsiders.)

There is a pair of *sandha*-words in the *Hevajra Tantra* that is particularly intriguing: *preksana* (the act of seeing) is *agati* (the act of arrival or achievement). In India the primary act of daily worship among Hindus is *darshana* (seeing): it is both a "viewing" of the gods as they are manifest inthe temple and wayside images, and something more: in *darshana* the eyes literally touch the gods; sight goes out to physically receive the god's blessing.

"Blanco" ends at the *chakra* between the eyes. Its last line reiterates an earlier couplet ("The unreality of the seen/ brings reality to seeing"*) in the context of a ritualized copulation: "Your body/ spilled on my body/ seen/ dissolved/ brings reality to seeing."**) The poem, then, never erases the world, never enters the "plentiful void" of *nirvana* (as the last canto of *Altazor* does: a void filled with syllable-seeds) or the "empty void" of *sunyata*. In the unreality of the world the poem ends by affirming the reality of a seeing which is touching which is writing. As Indian philosophy often reiterates, perception is real, even if what is perceived is unreal. [In the famous Buddhist parable, a man is frightened by a piece of rope lying on the ground which he thinks is a snake, runs away, trips, and breaks his leg: although the cause is unreal, the effect is not.]

Tantric art is notable for its representation of the cosmos in another form of simple or complex geometric drawing: the *yantra*. Paz's India (India's Paz) is a *yantra* composed of a triangle (seeing-touching-writing) within a square (body-world-cosmos-language) within a circle, which in India stands for a vision or a system. An O that is a poet's political button, this poet's monogram, the egg (symbol and syllable) of the cosmos, and the delineation of the nothing— the empty void or the plentiful void— from which everything is created and to which it returns.

In the *Hevajra Tantra*, in the rituals in which Buddhas and Masters, goddesses and yoginis dance, "the sound of a bee is heard at

La irrealidad de lo mirado/ da realidad a la mirada.

**Tu cuerpo/ derranmado en mi cuerpo/ visto/ desvanecido/ da realidad a la mirada.*

the end of the song": in *Blanco*, it is "this insect/ fluttering among these lines."*

In the meditation, the yogin imagines a lotus blossoming on his navel. On the petals of the lotus are the letters of the *mantra* ARHAN. Smoke appears, rising from the letter R. Suddenly a spark, a burst of flame, and the lotus is consumed by fire. The wind picks up and scatters the ashes, covering him from head to toe. Then a gentle rain falls, and slowly washed them away. Bathed, refreshed, the yogin sees his body shining like the moon.

Este insecto/ revoloteando entre estas palabras.

....

PAZ & BECKETT

[*Written as the introduction to* The Bread of Days: Eleven Mexican Poets,
Translated by Samuel Beckett, *a limited edition with artwork*
by Enrique Chagoya (Yolla Bolly Press), 1994.]

On the flowers the angel of the mist
scattered pearly moisture from his wings,
and Aurora floated on the air,
enveloped in her gauzy topaz robe.

It was the nuptial hour. The earth lay sleeping,
virginal, beneath the bashful veil,
and to surprise her with his amorous kisses
the royal sun inflamed the firmament.

Who would suspect that the officiants at this pastelled marriage of heaven and earth were none other than two of the primary architects of postwar international modernism? If part of the Surrealist project depended on the fortuitous conjunction of disparate elements in an unlikely place, then surely one of its oddest late productions was an unassuming book called *An Anthology of Mexican Poetry*. For far beyond its ostensible subject matter, the book was the result of an improbable encounter between Octavio Paz and Samuel Beckett on the field of classical Mexican literature.

In 1949, Beckett was forty-three and Paz thirty-five. Both were living in Paris, and both were generally broke. Beckett was trying to find a producer for his play, *Waiting for Godot*, and a publisher for *Molloy*, the first of his trilogy of novels. (His earlier novel, *Murphy*, had sold exactly six copies in its first year of publication.) Paz, though known in Mexico as a young poet, was just finishing the books that would propel his international reputation, *The Labyrinth of Solitude* and *The Bow and the Lyre*. His first major long poem, *Sunstone*, was still some years away.

Paz had a low-level position at the Mexican embassy. Beckett was surviving on literary hackwork, some of it for UNESCO, which was then sponsoring a series of representative works of world literature in translation. Beckett called it "that inexhaustible cheese," though his own life at the time, according to his biographer Deirdre Bair, was more rat than mouse: sleeping all day and roaming the streets of Paris all night.

The UNESCO cheese lured Paz into a project for which he had little enthusiasm: an anthology of Mexican poetry to be translated into French and English. Paz, an anti-nationalist, would have preferred to consider Spanish American poetry as a whole. And worse, in Mexico, between the twin volcanoes of the 17th and 20th century poetries lay a gloomy valley of some two hundred years of largely feeble European imitations.

The book was further encumbered when a well-known Mexican poet, Jaime Torres-Bodet, became the director of UNESCO Torres-Bodet, with the once-prevalent inferiority complex of the Third

World intellectual in the halls of European culture, insisted that each edition be introduced by one of those grandiloquent poohbahs who perennially serve the role as "leading critic." For the French edition, Torres-Bodet chose Paul Claudel, then eighty-one, decades past his best poetry, and largely preoccupied with theological questions. For the English, he asked Sir Cecil Maurice Bowra, the Hellenist and warden of Wadham College, Oxford. Neither had the least interest in Mexico. I've never seen Claudel's text, but Bowra's introduction, called "Poetry and Tradition," cheerfully rambles for pages through world poetry— not excluding that of the Ainu, the Asiatic Tartars, and the Lower Slovenians— until it final settles, in the third-to-last sentence, on the subject at hand. That sentence— Bowra's only comment on the matter— informs us that Mexico has a "vivid and varied culture."

Paz was, as he recalls, furious, and further disappointed when Torres Bodet decided that Alfonso Reyes, the Grand Old Man of Mexican letters, would be the only living poet admitted in the book. This meant eliminating the work of poets such as Xavier Villaurrutia and José Gorostiza, members of the *Contemporáneos* (Contemporaries), the vibrant and internationalist Mexican poetry group that flourished in the 1930's and 40's, and was so important to Paz's own writing.

Paz was responsible for finding the translators for the two editions. For the French he commissioned Guy Lévis Mano, a poet and Spanish translator who remains known as one of the great printers of the Surrealist movement, producing limited editions of texts by Breton, Tzara, Michaux, Char, and Soupault, with artwork by Giacometti, Picasso, Man Ray, Miró, and others. For the English, someone suggested Samuel Beckett, whom Paz knew slightly through their mutual publication in Max-Pol Fouchet's magazine *Fontaine*. An obstacle that would daunt lesser, or less hungry, mortals— Beckett's total ignorance of the Spanish language— was quickly overcome. Beckett had "a friend" who would help, and he had, after all, studied Latin at Trinity College. Beckett completed his work in March or April of 1950. The original manuscript, now in Texas, includes two pages of notes, "not in Beckett's hand," on the translation of specific words, as well as corrections and additions "mostly in another hand." (No one knows to whom these hands belonged.) The French edition was published in 1952 by Editions Nagel, had one printing, and vanished. The English language edition, delayed for unknown reasons until 1958, appeared simultaneously from Thames & Hudson in the U.K. and the Indiana University Press. Thanks in part to its unusual collaborators, it has remained in print in paperback ever since, an extraordinarily long publishing run for what is, after all, a collection of otherwise generally arcane texts.

Years later, Beckett would write that his work on the Mexican anthology was strictly an "alimentary chore," and that the poems were "execrable for the most part." And certainly those martinets of the bilingual dictionary who normally review poetry translations would have a field day with Beckett: In the poems included here, for example, he drops two lines from the López Velarde poem, and writes "twenty" for "seventy." He is hopelessly lost among Mexican flora and fauna, confusing macaws and macaques, tigers and jaguars, magueys and aloes. (When the going gets really rough, in Alfonso Reyes' "Tarahumara Herbs," he randomly selects Old World plants to stand in for the Mexican.) He's clearly unfamiliar with such things as the Mexican calendar stone, which he calls "a stone of sun." Sometimes he's mysterious, as when a *sinfonía lograda* (a fully-realized symphony) becomes a "symphony of positive esthetics." Sometimes, he's just being Beckett, as when the last lines of Rodríguez Galván's poem (which mean, literally, "Dream, be my passage through the world,/ until that new dream, sweet and graceful,/ shows me the sublime face of God.") are clipped to "Dream, in thy safe keeping let me come/ to this world's end..." (Even in a translation, Godot can never arrive.) And in many of the poems he seems to be on autopilot, cruising until he can reach the next poem.

Yet Beckett's Mexican anthology is one of the liveliest English translations of the century. Its greatest achievement is its recreation of that sense of reading old texts, the distance between us and them. (One has it in one's own language, but rarely in translation, which tends to be written according to present-day usage, whatever present-day it is.) Beckett accomplishes this through a subtle mimicking— and who, besides Joyce, was a better mimic?—of the English poetry contemporary to whatever period he is translating. And he displays a stupefyingly vast command of English archaicisms that will send any diligent reader deep into the OED. In the poems included here, we find, among others, "grateless" for ungrateful; "cramoisy" for crimson; "featly" for graceful; "ensample" for example; "cark" for anxiety or grief; "adust" for scorched; "flower-de-luce" for iris; "monachal" for monastic; "fatidic" for prophetic; "tilths" for tillable land; "popinjay" for parrot; "mede" for recompense; as well as "chalchuite"— an archaic derivative from the Nahuatl word *chalchihuite*— for turquoise. In two cases, even the OED didn't help: "wildering" for wandering; and a bird's "crawy" call. Did Beckett make them up, did someone misread his notorious crabbed handwriting, or are these actually lacunae in the definitive dictionary? With Beckett's erudition, one never knows: I thought "gyps" was a typographical error for "gypsum" until I discovered it was an obsolete form. And I was puzzled that he would translate "pheasant" as "bird of Phasis"— not knowing that the word derives from the Phasis river where the birds once abounded.

Moreover, he has created a vivid music for each poem by avoiding the end-rhymes of the Spanish (while still suggesting the original prosody through complex internal rhymes) and by breaking the lines where the English, not the original, demands it. He can take a sow's ear, like the opening two lines of Nervo's "An Old Burden," and turn it, if not quite to silk, then into a purse with some inner compartments. Nervo's lines mean, literally:

Who is that siren with the voice so painful.
with flesh so white, with braids/tresses so dark brown?

Beckett transforms this to:

Who is yonder siren so distressed
of voice, so white of flesh, so dark of tress?

The "yonder" may be a bit much, but the rhymes of "distressed," "flesh," and "tress" are more complex than the original, which doesn't rhyme at all. The poem sings, as it doesn't in Spanish. And the play between "distressed" and "tress," which Beckett made up, no doubt made his day's (or night's) work more amusing.

There are whole poems, such as the Nervo, that strike me as better in English than Spanish, and quite a few individual lines are simply more intense in the translation:

greeny sea-wrack coils a snaky tress
(Balbuena)

209

In such throng of dead forms thou didst not die
                    (Sandoval y Zapata)

Space is azure and the mountains bathe
in vivid azure and in azure shade
                    (Rodríguez Galván)

For the people the bard is grace not cark
                    (Díaz Mirón)

A precious pearl in the slaver of a mollusc
                    (Díaz Mirón)

and throughout that brooding and adust
savannah, not a path, not a track
                    (Othón)

what a wildering midst ruins and pits!
                    (Othón)

and many books made me all-ignorant
                    (González Martínez)

or the Yeatsian:

the tower riddled in the slinging winds
                    (López Velarde)

We will never know whether Beckett, despite later denials, was
secretly enchanted with some of the poems, or whether, with a
writer like Beckett, his hackwork would be anybody else's master-

piece. But no matter how or why it was written, forty-five years later the book still remains the best introduction in English to classical Mexican poetry, and the repository of some remarkable poems. It stands, in some strange way, next to that other great, late 1940's invention of Mexico in English, *Under the Volcano*.

Certainly it is as impossible to imagine Beckett in Mexico as it is to imagine Malcolm Lowry anywhere else. And yet one wonders if there was not a shock of recognition when Beckett read the first page of the manuscript Paz gave him. It contained what is perhaps the first sonnet written in Mexico, by the first Mexican Spanish poet, Francisco de Terrazas. Had Beckett never translated Mexican poetry, we might never have made the connection. But because of his presence, a curious loop forms. For Mexican poetry begins not in the expected grand and tragic spectacle of the Conquest, but with a single individual in a desolate landscape, a nobody suffering in nowhere, that dismal world for which Beckett, centuries later, would be the great cartographer:

I dreamed that I was thrown from a crag
by one who held my will in servitude,
and all but fallen to the griping jaws
of a wild beast in wait for me below.

In terror, gropingly, I cast around
for wherewith to uphold me with my hands,
and the one closed about a trenchant sword,
and the other twined about a little herb.

Little and little the herb came swift away,
and the sword ever sorer vexed my hand
as I more fiercely clutched its cruel edges...

Oh wretched me, and how from self estranged,
that I rejoice to see me mangled thus
for dread of ending, dying, my distress!

YUGOSLAVIA

[*Written for an issue of* Global City Review *devoted to texts of two*
pages or less, 1994. An attempt to discover what, if anything,
could be said in a few words about an enormity.]

Yugoslavia, you open a newspaper, charred at the edges, riddled with holes. Two men in suits walk down the sidewalk, chatting, oblivious to the elderly woman lying shot dead at their feet. A severed head on a pile of shoes. You. It's you. Yugoslavia.

War and always war, but certain wars seem evidence of something more than the varieties of human brutality. Certain small wars, seen from a distance that turns their daily horror into allegory: another, bloodless war that is reenacted in the mind, our minds, we who are not in the slaughter. Wars one can't stop thinking about. As if the way they, over there, are dying is a reflection of the way we are living. And worse: that the way we are living is the cause of their dying.

Until now, Spain, in this century, was the small internal war that unravelled transnationally as a parable of the age. Not only as the first performance, in a provincial "theater of war," of the global cataclysmic battle against fascism: Spain, in Western minds, was the triumph of the destroyers of art, and of the tech-

213

nologically powerful over the aspirations of ordinary people. "Guernica," the painting, draws its force, not from its depiction of carnage— there is always carnage— but from the image of the old ways being oliterated by what is most horrible in the new ways. The airplane— till then the great symbol and glory of the Machine Age— brings not the reign of progress, but a rain of bombs. It is a scene that was reenacted from the conquest of the Americas to the last of the colonial wars: Algeria, Vietnam, Angola. What we, the "modern" people, most hate about ourselves is the agent of the destruction of what we imagine is most admirable in the "old" people, the people we think we once were.

These are wars that seem, for the moment, over: the imperial territorial expansions, the wars in the name of this century's cruel ideologies, the aspirations of a peasantry hopelessly crushed by the technologically advanced. Instead we have the so-called "tribal" wars: the revivals, manipulated by the power-hungry, of supposedly ancient ethnic, racial, religious animosities. Wars, we are told, that return to the roots of war.

But these are not wars taking place in the rain forest, or even in the Balkans in the years before the First World War. These are wars being acted out within a global network of communication, and within a global consumer market. The dead are seen "live," all over the planet, on the television news; the combatants, on either side, drink the same Coca-Cola. The world is simultaneously coming together and blowing apart, the "steady state" model of the universe.

Yugoslavia— ex-Yugoslavia— above all, is the emblem of the age, and not merely as the chaos that follows the collapse of empires and ideologies. Yugoslavia is a nervous breakdown in the collective mind of the West.

Sick and weary at the end of a century that murdered millions in the name of certainty, the generation that considers itself "post"— post-modern,post-ideology— has, in an unprecedented, nearly unbelievable manner, transformed doubt into a science. After three centuries, the Age of Criticism has reached its decadence. Words do not mean what they say; books are lies imagined into truth by their readers; images are the representation of a conspiracy between creators and receptor; every narrative is false, and any opposing notion equally true. It is a dismantling of the world, they say, so that murderous certainty will never happen again.

As always, what will never happen happens over. The tragedy of Yugoslavia is the certainty of the combatants, and the paralyzing uncertainty of the rest who are watching. There, people die every day in the name of their belief, and continue to die every day in the name of our disbelief. Here, we see the evidence, and wonder what is evidence, and wonder what to do, and wonder in what name is anything done, and let a thousand other images rush in.

[4 March 1994]

THE REVOLUTION AT ST. MARK'S CHURCH

[In May 1994 the Poetry Project at St. Mark's Church in New York held its annual symposium; the topic that year was "Revolutionary Poetry."

On the opening night there were four "keynote" speakers: Erica Hunt, an African-American poet and labor organizer; Eileen Myles, poet and gay activist; Amiri Baraka; and, inexplicably, myself.

The evening began strangely: As I entered the church, a young woman from the Project said, "Oh, we got your package and paid for it." She handed me a bulging jiffy bag that had been sent to me care of the church, C.O.D. for $27.

I couldn't help but open it. The package was filled with trash.

Hunt spoke first; in the subsequent chaos I'm afraid I've forgotten what she said. Then I spoke; the reception did not seem particularly hostile. Myles gave a very funny "I'm a lesbian" rap. Baraka got up, talked for five minutes, then whipped out his notebook, said, "And now I'd like to reply to the gentleman who proceeded me," and launched into a fifteen-minute tirade, pointing his finger at me. No one expresses rage like Amiri Baraka— a rage that has also led to indelible poetry. When he turned to Myles, shouting that lesbianism has nothing to do with the revolution, she began yelling back.

Things fell apart, and the night ended.

A few months later, Poetry Flash ran an account of the symposium by Tim Griffin. He wrote: "Everyone seemed to be hating Eliot Weinberger, who attempted to derail

the notion of an effective 'witness poetry,' and espoused what scholar
Walter Lew would in a panel discussion the next daycall 'an incredibly outdated
liberal, Cold War demonization of China.' Baraka had kicked his two cents in
against Weinberger as well, saying that revolution never consisted of 'an endowed
chair in a concentration camp.'" This was followed by a report in the
Poetry Project newsletter by Douglas Rothschild on my "now legendary talk."
Rothschild held up Jackson Mac Low as "living proof" against "Mr. Weinberger's
claim that politically radical views & allegiances lead you to stop writing."
And he wrote that "Mr. Baraka had taken very careful notes on what
Mr. Weinberger had just said & launched a full scale barrage; effectively
scuttling Mr. Weinberger's thesis (the likes of which we have not seen
since the Potempkin) [sic]."
I wrote to the newsletter in an attempt to salvage what I'd actually said, to
remind them that the Potemkin sailors were the Good Guys, and to wonder why
neither of the correspondents had been alarmed by, among other things,
Baraka's condemnation of the "pornography" of rap lyrics, and his defense
of the imprisonment of the utterly apolitical but gay writer Reinaldo Arenas
as a "counter-revolutionary." This led to a letter in a subsequent issue
from Baraka, with three variations in seven sentences of the line
"bourgeois intellectuals like Weinberger lie."
It's curious that this corner of Po-World was scandalized, and thought they were
hearing neocon ravings— one person called it "the Pentagon version of world
poetry"— when actually I had uttered a series of banal commonplaces. Many
in the audience were infants during the Vietnam War. It was disheartening
that they had grown up to adopt uncritically the specific dreams and models
of Revolution that are now— particularly in the countries where they once
occurred— almost kitsch.

The speech was, of course, intended to be heard, not read. It should be noted again that this is May 1994: in retrospect, a calm before the storm. Within the next year, the U.S. would see the ascension of Gingrich (to call him Newt is to insult our salamander friends), the passage of Proposition 187 in California, the Republican feeding frenzy on the poor, and the Oklahoma bombing. —July 1995]

....

Lenin to Maxim Gorki: "I can't listen to music too often. It affects your nerves, makes you want to say nice stupid things and stroke the heads of people who could create such beauty while living in this vile hell. These days you mustn't stroke anyone's head— you might get your hand bitten off. You have to hit them on the head, without any mercy."

There is something nostalgic and quaint, and something sickening, about a conference now, in 1994, on revolutionary poetry. [My first thought, on being invited here, was to recall the least prophetic line uttered in my lifetime: "The revolution will not be televised."] And yet the subject is more pertinent than ever. I want to clear through the first, to get to the second.

First, a matter of definitions, the classic difference between revolt and revolution. Revolt is an uprising of some kind against some aspect of the existing order. Revolution is the struggle, nearly always, but not necessarily, a violent struggle, to replace one form of society and state with another. Most important, the form of the new society is usually fairly fixed in the minds of the revolutionaries. In this sense, nearly all of us in the generation of 1968— except Bill & Hillary— were engaged in some form of

218

revolt; but only a few were revolutionaries. It's always a mistake to confuse one with the other, particularly as revolutionary societies tend to suppress any further revolt.

In talking about revolutionary poetry— in its political sense— I also want to draw a line between it and political, "socially aware" poetry. The poetry that bears witness to, or expresses outrage at, or is the product of, the enormous horrors and injustices of the historical moment is not necessarily revolutionary. It is only revolutionary when it serves, in some way, the destruction of the old order, and carries within it a formed image of the new order. Traditionally, revolutionary poetry presents the horrific details of present existence, excoriates or lampoons those who are responsible for the misery, rallies its readers or listeners to struggle against injustice, exalts certain individual heroes of that struggle, and offers a vision of the paradise that will follow the victory of the revolutionary forces.

Politically revolutionary poetry only sometimes coincides with aesthetically revolutionary poetry. When it does, we have some of the great poetry of the century: Hikmet, Neruda, MacDiarmid, Brecht, Mayakovsky, to name a few. When it doesn't— as is obvious when one reads old issues of the *New Masses* or any anthology of guerrilla poetry— it can produce some of the worst poetry, some of it written by these same poets: a poetry where the message is the medium.

But the real problem with revolutionary poetry is the Revolution. With certain exceptions— Mexico, Spain, Iran, among them— nearly every important revolution of the 20th century has been fought under the inspiration of Karl Marx. [Though interestingly, none of these revolutions were imagined by Marx, and were, in fact, specifically denied by him: He believed that the revolution would be led by the urban proletariat in countries like

England and Germany, and thought that a revolution led by the rural peasantry, in a place like Russia, would be impossible. Furthermore, he assumed an internationalism to the revolutionary proletariat, quite unlike the nationalistic Marxist revolutions that actually occurred.]

I happen to think that all of us as writers, like any good union members, must judge the merits of a state first according to what it does for (or against) us as writers. And there is no question that, in this respect, all of the Communist states were, or continue to be, disasters. On the one hand, Communism brought nearly universal literacy to its masses and produced millions of inexpensive books for them to read; it created writers' unions where the state essentially paid writers to write. On the other hand, these same states all enforced strict censorship, and tended to execute, imprison, exile or silence most of their best writers. The writers who flourished were either supporters who were famous before the revolution, achieving a kind of Grand Old Man status (such as Nicolás Guillén or Alejo Carpentier in Cuba) or else they were the kind of utter mediocrities— familiar to us in the U.S. or any capitalist country— who thrive in arts bureaucracies.

How thrilling it once seemed that Chairman Mao wrote poetry in classical Chinese— even though no one else was allowed to do the same, akind of poet's dream. In China, the revolution wiped out a thriving modernist movement that had begun in the 1920's and 30's. The poets who were not killed were essentially required to write useful paeans to the boiler plate factories. Only in the crevices could something new or aesthetically radical be published: translations of foreign poets with impeccable political credentials, such as Neruda, Eluard or Lorca, or considered too remote in time to be dangerous, such as Rimbaud and Baudelaire. It was these translations that inspired the young poets who came of age in the Cultural Revolution and rejected social realism to write what were, at first, simple, highly subjective imagist poems. In the 1970's, a whole generation of students was exhilarated by a line of poetry most of us in the West would be too embarrassed to write: Bei Dao's "I— do— not— believe!" For in a collective society, what is more subversive than the first-person singular, a negative and a verb? Targeted by the "anti-spiritual pollution" campaign, these poets were imprisoned, silenced, or forced to publish underground. Since the Tiananmen Square massacre in 1989, most of them are in exile.

How thrilling it once was that Che carried a copy of Neruda's *Heights of Macchu Picchu* in his knapsack in Bolivia. Meanwhile, in Cuba, a poet as great as Neruda, José Lezama Lima, was under a form of house arrest, and forbidden to publish. Today, when I think of Cuba, it is not all the beautiful books published by Casa de las Americas. It is one writer among the many exiles: Reinaldo Arenas, who spent a few years in prison for the crime of being homosexual, who wrote novels that were confiscated and then wrote them out again, and who was finally let out of the country with the mentally retarded and the violent criminals in the Mariel boat exodus. It is Arenas, some years before he began dying of AIDS, in a tenement in Times Square, telling me, with serious intensity, that the KGB had some sort of death ray aimed at his apartment, and that it had exploded a glass of water on his windowsill.

How thrilling it was to read about Nicaragua under the Sandinistas, proclaimed here as a "land of poets," with a well-known poet, Ernesto Cardenal, as its Minister of Culture, who had opened hundreds of poetry workshops around the country for the *campesinos*. No one seemed to remember that Cardenal had started out as the youngest member of the Nicaraguan poet *vanguardia*, fascists who supported Franco, Mussolini, and the first Somoza, and that Cardenal himself wrote love poems to one of the Somoza girls. That his conversion to both Marx and the Church had led to some strange conjunctions, as when, in one of his many poems against the Vietnam War, he compared napalm to abortion. Of all the American poets who trooped down to Nicaragua in those years, how many reported back that in the workshops only a certain kind of poetry, called "exteriorism," could be written, and that, among other things, traditional prosody and all metaphors were strictly forbidden? How many reported back that gays and lesbians who had fought for the revolution were interrogated and sometimes imprisoned in an attempt to purge the Sandinista ranks of deviants?

I need hardly speak of the Soviet Union and Eastern Europe, where, as Mandelstam said, they took poetry seriously. But it is revealing that those poets who maintained a life-long devotion to the Party tended to live incountries that never had a Communist government— Neruda, Vallejo, Aragon, Eluard, MacDiarmid, Césaire, among many others— or else, like Brecht and others in Eastern Europe, had never experienced a revolution. For what Communism governments understood too well is that a collective builds a dam, but a book can only be the result of a subversive solitude.

The landscape of the revolution is filled with doomed young people. Here is Roque Dalton, the guerrilla saint of Latin America:

The Party must train the poet as a good militant Communist, as a valuable cadre for mass revolutionary action. The poet must contribute in the utmost to the cultural education of all members of the Party. The Party, specifically, must help the poet develop into an effective agitator, a soldier with expert marksmanship—

in a word, a fit cadre. The poet must acquaint all his com-
rades with Nazim Hikmet or Pablo Neruda, and give them a
clear concept of the role of cultural work within the context of
general revolutionary activity. He must also make sure that the
Administrative Secretary of the Central Committee, for example,
loves St. John of the Cross, Henri Michaux, or St-John Perse.

Dalton joined the People's Revolutionary Army (ERP) in his native El Salvador. In 1975, unattracted by possible discussions of *Anabasis* or *Miserable Miracle*, he was executed by his own people as a CIA spy. (This is now attributed to a "militarist" or "adventurist" or "Maoist" faction.) A few years later, the ERP-formed the Roque Dalton Cultural Brigade.

Doomed young people: The great unwritten history in 20th century American poetry is the black hole into which the young poets vanished inthe 1930's. In 1931 Louis Zukofsky attempted to launch a new generation of American modernist poets with his "Objectivist's" issue of *Poetry* and subsequent anthology. The fate of four of these "Objectivists" is well known: Zukofsky would not publish his first pamphlet of poetry for another ten years; Oppen's second book came 28 years after his first; Rakosi took 26 years between books; Reznikoff, who was not a young man in the 30's, like William Carlos Williams and the young poet Kenneth Fearing, essentially gave up poetry during the late 30's and 40's to write prose. These four survived, after long periods of not writing or not publishing, but most of the other young poets included as "Objectivists" were never heard from again. Other anthologies from the period are similarly filled with the disappeared. In fact, the only significant poet to start publishing in book form in the 1930's and keep publishing was Muriel Rukeyser— with Kenneth Patchen a distant second— and

Rukeyser, throughout her career, inhabited a no-man's zone between the avant-garde and the establishment, modernism and agit-prop.

[This was also true of prose writers: We know that some of the most prominent, such as Dos Passos and James T. Farrell, ended up as disillusioned cranks in the pages of the *National Review*. As for the others: in an interview just a few weeks ago, Henry Roth— who himself stopped publishing for 60 years— wondered what happened to the scores of writers he knew as a young radical.]

This was the period in America when the Party dominated intellectual life. I don't mean to suggest that all of the poets, like Oppen, joined the Party and gave up writing for organizing, though some undoubtedly did. Rather I think it was the general discourse fostered by the Party that discouraged young poets from going on. This was the era— to take Camus' example— when young people hotly debated whether one served the people best by being Shakespeare or a shoemaker, whether a pair of sturdy shoes was worth all the plays of Shakespeare, and whether, in Brecht's famous formulation, it was a crime, in times like these, to talk about trees. Who could write poetry when one had to defend both the utilitarianism of poetry and the murder of poets for the greater good? Only the stubborn, the oblivious, or those who had begun writing before Stalin. And who can keep writing, who can age gracefully, as it becomes apparent that there is nothing more unreal than yesterday's realism?

In retrospect, there is only one major world poet who managed to keep his commitment to Communism, keep writing, and never write a line of doggerel: César Vallejo. His solution was to churn out colorless Party-hack prose and keep the poetry utterly uncontaminated, free to do whatever he wished: a prose to serve the people, and a poetry to serve poetry. Not coincidentally, it may be the most political, and the most revolutionary, poetry ever written by a Latin American— a poetry not only written out of extreme poverty and the trashheap of history, but one that dismantled and reinvented the received language of the conquistadors.

Three fundamentalisms have dominated the revolutions of this century: Marxism, fascism, and Islam. (The fundamentalisms of the other two monotheisms have created states, but not modern revolutions.) Because of this, it has become impossible to talk about revolutionary poetry, or the revolution itself, without reference to them. And the fact remains that, from Nazi Germany to Iran to Kampuchea— or, right at this moment, from Algeria to North Korea— they have murdered, imprisoned or silenced hundreds, probably thousands of poets, as the so-called secular capitalist states, with all their injustices, have never done. No amount of revolutionary romanticism, of the kind that is still being written, can obscure this. Now matter how thrilling, how inspiring to the poets revolution can be, the message is plain: After the revolution, you'd better move somewhere else.

What we need is a revolution of revolutions, a revolution to crush the dreams of the old revolutions and construct new ones, a revolution that will tear down the monoliths and not build prisons in their place, a revolution that will honor continual revolt, a revolution where the poets can live in their own homes. Who knows what that revolution could be? For the moment, it may only be possible to imagine what it will be pitched against.

Two specters haunt the next century. One is the secularism, nationalism, and ethnocentricity, the psychological apartheid that is paradoxically erupting as the world moves toward a single consumer culture. The other is the very real possibility of the extinction of the human race, following the extinction of countless other species. Overpopulation, deforestation, the nuclear weapons that are still very much with us, the rotting canisters of plutonium on the ocean floor— I need hardly recite the list. We are at a moment in history when it is a crime not to talk about trees.

A revolution against these demons would require the kind of Internationale that Marx dreamed of, and Communism never saw— a rising of the humans of the world. It would depend on a transition to a global economy that is simultaneous to a dismantling of the multinational corporations. And it must begin with us talking to each other— more important, listening to each other— in ways that have never occurred before. Significantly, with the new information technology, the means are there— as long as we are able to keep those means democratic, and out of monopolistic control, which won't be easy. The new generation of revolutionaries will not begin as a ragged band in the sierras— it will be individuals and small groups thousands of miles from each other and neighbors in cyberspace.

And where are the poets in all this? First, as has been often said, revolutionaries are connoisseurs of the apocalypse and visionaries of the terrestrial paradise. Poets, though not lately in America, have always excelled at both. So we need poets to challenge received notions, tell us what we don't know, ask the questions we can't answer, and wake us up to both doom and Utopia.

Second, poetry has always traveled on its own Internet of underground channels from country to country. These must multiply, especially in the United States, which seems more self-preoccupied than ever. The 90's, beginning as they did in 1989, have brought extraordinary changes all over the world— many of them exhilarating, and many of them achieved without violence. Meanwhile, as you've probably noticed, absolutely nothing is happening here, in Anno 14 of Reagan America. We'd be better off if every member of the government resigned tomorrow, and was replaced by a citizen picked at random. And the left, such as it is, is obsessed with a new form of nationalism called multiculturalism—which is healthy insofar as it brings more Americans into the dialogue, and sick in that it still excludes everyone else: Chinese-Americans and no Chinese, African-Americans and no Africans, Mexican-Americans and no Mexicans. Only one contemporary Chinese poet has had books published in the U.S., no Indians writing in Indian languages, one or two Africans, maybe half a dozen Latin Americans, one Arab poet, a few from the Caribbean. The current poetry of 85% of humanity is represented in this country by a one-foot shelf of books. Americans, and American poets specifically, may be the last people to get the word that it's global time. Even the speakers and panelists all weekend here, at this symposium on an international theme, are a United Colors of strictly Americans.

Finally, I think we have to assert, over and over, that the revolution of the world requires many revolutions of the word, and that poetry does indeed make something happen, no matter how slowly it moves from reader to reader. Zbigniew Herbert has written that the fire in the poem is one thing, and the town in flames another. In a sense of course it's true, but in another sense, it is the fire in the poem that helps us to see the town in flames, whether it is a town in history, or our own town tomorrow. Poetry is a way— not the only way, but for most of us here, our way— into the enormous events of history. Only bad poetry talks to itself, or tells us what we already know. Above all, only bad poetry is not subversive. The revolution will not only be televised, it will be read.

MY PET RABBIT

I had a pet rabbit that developed a dental problem. Its upper and lower incisors did not meet to grind each other down, and they kept growing. If left unattended, as sometimes happens in the wild, the teeth will grow to such length that they curve back into the rabbit's skull and pierce the brain. The veterinarian told me to buy a pair of special podiatrist's scissors and regularly clip the teeth.

The first time I tried, I botched the job. The teeth shattered; there was a lot of blood. An hour later I had to take a plane to another country, to attend one of those cultural conventions, always held abroad, where foreign governments treat otherwise obscure intellectuals to exorbitant hospitality.

I was met at the airport by an official, ushered to the front of the immigration line, and taken in a limousine to an elegant hotel. That night, in a suite on the fortieth floor, looking over the radiant expanse of an endless city, alone in a bed vast as that city, I couldn't sleep. The memory of the rabbit's bloody mouth kept me staring out the window.

The next morning another limousine took me, a French poet, and a Chinese painter for a visit to a provincial capital. I already knew the place, so while the others toured the cathedral, I went to find a junk store on the Street of Frogs where, years before, I had bought a small, rusty mechanical device whose function no one has been able to ascertain.

Walking the colonial streets, I came across a crowd of a few hundred people and some television crews milling about, apparently waiting for something. I had read in the local paper that the students had been protesting some university action; I assumed that the crowd was waiting for a demonstration march to pass by. Half of the block was deserted. The crowd on either side had formed its own barriers, in order, I thought, to keep the sight-lines clear for the cameras. There were no police, no agitation, nothing more than the familiar sight of a large group in the semi-comatose state of waiting.

A tourist, I was following a map, and my map told me that the shortest distance to where I was going was across the no-man's-land of the empty half-block. I crossed unhurriedly. People on either side began waving frantically, perhaps, I thought, because I was stumbling into what was to be the television picture. Then there was the crack of a shot, and I saw the brick wall near my head chip. Unalarmed, barely registering the event, not reacting with the "fight or flight" supposedly programmed in my genes, I quickened my pace, but did not run, toward the crowd on the other side. The next day I read that a student group was occupying the building; a rival group was trying to take it from them; the first group had placed snipers on the roof; two people had been shot that day.

The rabbit was all right. Its teeth resumed growing, and I periodically clipped with increasing expertise. Months later, I woke gasping, in the first asthma attack of my life. Tests showed that I was violently allergic to rabbits; the rabbit stayed to mollify the children; the asthma continued. One night that summer, at a house in the country, a Siberian husky belonging to a neighbor smashed through the small cage where the rabbit was living out-doors, mauled it to death, and then couldn't get out.

I thought of my pet rabbit a few years later, after reading, in an academic journal, a review of a book of mine that ended, "Weinberger simply needs a freshman English class." Never having had a freshman English class, I decided to write an essay titled "My Pet Rabbit"; it seemed the thing to do. I sent it to a friend who sometimes teaches creative writing. She thought the essay was vague and pointless, and that if I was trying to draw a parallel between myself and the rabbit as victims, it wasn't very clear. This connection had never occurred to me. But it was true that the various cruelties of the story, deliberate and inadvertent, large and small, had all, by the fact of their isolation in my writing of it, become linked, even portentous. This was not what I had intended and, discouraged, I abandoned the essay titled "My Pet Rabbit."

[1995]

....

NAKED MOLE-RATS

Naked mole-rats have no fur, but their lips are hairy. Their pinkish mottled skin is loose and hangs in folds, like something that has lost a great deal of weight, the easier to squirm through their narrow tunnels. Incisors protrude from their mouths like pincers, the only feature of their undefined faces. One naked mole-rat can fit across your fingers, its tail dangling down. They have been under the earth for at least three million years.

They never surface. They are blind. Their world is not a labyrinth, but a straight tunnel, a mile or two long, with innumerable cul-de-sacs branching off, and certain larger chambers. They live on the tuberous roots that grow towards them.

As many as three hundred inhabit a colony, moving a ton of dirt every month. They have a caste system, tripartite like the Indian. The smallest among them are the diggers and food-gatherers who work through the night in a line, male and female equally, the first gnawing the earth and kicking it back to the next who kicks it back, until the last, who digs a temporary hole to the surface, kicks out the dirt, its rump exposed to the moon and predators, and then plugs the hole again. When they come across a root, they chew off pieces to carry to the others.

The medium-sized are the warriors, who try to fend off the rufous-beaked snakes, the file snakes, the white-lipped snakes and the sand boas that sometimes find their way in. They attack with repeated tiny bites that are, if the snake is small enough, mysteriously instantly fatal. When, bychance, two colonies of naked mole-rats tunnel into each other, their warriors fight to the death.

These castes serve the largest, who are the breeders. Unique among mammals, only one female reproduces. She is by far the longest and the fattest and the most aggressive in the colony. If she dies there is chaos. She is attended by one to three males, who do nothing else. They spend their time nuzzling her; have sex, initiated by her, by mounting her from behind for fifteen seconds, bracing themselves by holding their front legs against the walls of the tunnel, and mainly failing. When she becomes pregnant, the teats of every colony member, male and female, enlarge, reach their peak at the birth, and then shrink. Just before birth, the female runs wildly through the tunnels.

She has four or five litters a year of a dozen pups. The babies have transparent skin through which their internal organs are clearly visible. Only a few survive, and they live long lives, twenty years or more. The dead babies are eaten, except for their heads. At times the live ones are eaten too.

Interbred so long, they are virtually clones. One dead-end branch of the tunnel is their toilet: they wallow there in the soaked earth so that all will smell alike. They are nearly always touching each other, rubbing noses, pawing, nuzzling. When their tunnel is blocked they work from both sides and reconnect it perfectly. They sleep in a packed heap in the nesting chamber, with the breeders on the top, staying warm, each naked mole-rat with its nose pressed against the anus and genitals of another.

They are continually cruel in small ways, clanking teeth, breathing rapidly into each other's open mouths, batting, swiping, biting, pulling one another's baggy skin, shoving each other sometimes a yard down the tunnel. But only the females who compete for the role of breeder inflict real harm. Wounded, the defeated female crouches shivering in the toilet, ignored by the others until she dies.

The tunnels are never silent. Naked mole-rats make at least seventeen sounds: soft chirps and loud chirps, high-pitched and low, tooth-grinding, trills, twitters, tongue-taps, sneezes, screams, hisses, grunts. Different sounds for when they bump into each other, when they piss, when they mate, when they're disturbed, alarmed, wounded, when they shove each other, when they meet a foreigner such as a beetle, when they find food, when they can't find food.

They clean their feet with their teeth. They clean their teeth with their feet. They yawn. They shiver. They scratch themselves after they piss. They bask near the surface, in the warm sunless earth. They doze with their short legs splayed, their huge heads drooping. They double over, mouth to anus, to eat their own shit.

They scurry with eyes closed, forwards or backwards at the same speed, over and under each other. They change direction by somersaulting. They find their way, when they don't know it, by darting forward till their nose bumps the wall, dart backwards, adjust the angle, dart forward again. Sometimes a naked mole-rat will suddenly stop, stand on its hind-legs and remain motionless, its head pressed against the roof of the tunnel. Above its head is the civil war in Somalia. Their hearing is acute.

[1995]

233

INDEX

INDEX

Irving Wallace 49
Sylvia Townsend Warner 156
Robert Penn Warren 188
R. Gordon Wasson 140-142
Vernon Watkins 20, 81
Burton Watson 80
Barrett Watten 85, 86, 89
Evelyn Waugh 68
Wei Hung 25
Alexis Weissenberg 47, 48
Phillip Whalen 20
Walt Whitman 15, 53, 116, 158
Benjamin Lee Whorf 89, 150
Richard Wilbur 81, 178, 188
Wendell Wilkie 180
Nancy Willard 187
Jonathan Williams 61, 62
William Carlos Williams 15, 53,
    62, 63, 77, 80, 83, 101, 125, 171,
    176, 182, 185, 188, 223
Edmund Wilson 86
Sir James Wilson 151
Yvor Winters 184
Christa Wolf 169
Stefan Wolpe 56
William Wordsworth 14, 73, 99
Charles Wright 187
James Wright 81, 188
Eleanor Wylie 184, 188

Xie Ye 173, 174

Yang Lian 173
W.B. Yeats 2, 31, 80, 157

David Young 187
Vernon Young 27, 28, 32

Ossip Zadkine 56
Marya Zaturenska 184
Louis Zukofsky 20, 77, 79, 81, 83,
    85, 89, 91, 176, 184, 186, 187,
    223

ABOUT THE AUTHOR

Eliot Weinberger is a noted essayist, translator, and editor. His essays on Asia, Latin America, poetry, and politics are collected in *Works on Paper* and *Outside Stories*, both published by New Directions. He is the co-author, with Octavio Paz, of a study of Chinese poetry translation, *Nineteen Ways of Looking at Wang Wei* (Moyer Bell), and the editor of the recent anthology *American Poetry Since 1950: Innovators & Outsiders* (Marsilio). Among his many translations of Latin American poetry and prose are the *Collected Poems of Octavio Paz 1957-1987* (New Directions), Vicente Huidobro's *Altazar* (Graywolf), Jorge Luis Borges's *Seven Nights* (New Directions), and Xavier Villaurrutia's *Nostalgia for Death* (Copper Canyon). In 1992, he was named the first recipient of the PEN/Kolovakos Award for his work in promoting Hispanic literature in the United States.